"Every church wants an effecti[illegible] one is easier said than done. It [illegible] in *Build on Jesus*, Deepak Reju and [illegible] Machowski distill decades of experience into a practical guide for building a culture marked by excellence and molded by gospel grace. As a new pastor, I am immensely grateful for this resource and will be handing it to every children's ministry leader at our church."

Matt Smethurst, Managing Editor, The Gospel Coalition; planting pastor, River City Baptist Church, Richmond, VA; author of *Deacons* and *Before You Open Your Bible*

"In a post-Christian environment, we must not be casual about evangelizing and discipling the next generation. The need is urgent. I assure you the enemy is not casual in his intent to wound and destroy our children. This book is already helping me refocus and reprioritize how we love and lead the precious children in our church to a rich, vibrant faith in Jesus."

Bob Lepine, Teaching Pastor, Redeemer Community Church, Little Rock, AR; cohost of *FamilyLife Today*

"Deepak and Marty's *Build on Jesus* is a great foundational resource for building a Christ-centered children's ministry. Theologically astute and sensible, this book is a great summary of what children's ministry should be all about. Applying these principles will help your children grow in Christian discipleship in a safe environment. The appendices are extremely helpful in developing a child protection policy that will ensure that your church is equipped to care for the most vulnerable in your congregation: your children."

Jeff Dalrymple, Executive Director, Evangelical Council for Abuse Prevention

"Deepak and Marty share a message that resonates deeply, one that the church needs to hear more than ever: children matter and so does children's ministry. *Build on Jesus* is weighty yet accessible, comprehensive yet succinct. From the purpose of children's ministry, to leadership roles, to ways to teach and protect children, this book provides ideal help for those new to ministry and is a valuable refresher for those who are seasoned."

Brian Dembowczyk, Managing Editor of *The Gospel Project*; author of *Cornerstones: 200 Questions and Answers to Learn Truth* and *Gospel-Centered Kids Ministry*

"When I was a children's and family pastor, I benefited greatly from Marty and Deepak's biblical resources, and I highly recommend *Build on Jesus*. This isn't one of those pragmatic, entertainment-driven, or church growth kinds of books. It's a doctrinally strong, biblically-based, gospel-centered guide by two experienced shepherds that is well worth your time. If you are involved in children's ministry, then you need to buy this book. Better yet, buy three copies and give one to your team and senior pastor. You will be glad you did!"

Josh Mulvihill, Author of *50 Things Every Child Needs to Know Before Leaving Home*

"Written by two seasoned family pastors, *Build on Jesus* is a perceptive portrayal of the blessings and challenges of ministry to children. Their book is engaging and replete with wise counsel gleaned from real life situations. This much-needed book will help children's ministry leaders set priorities, care for the people in children's ministry, and find practical guidance."

David and Sally Michael, Cofounders of Truth78

"*Build on Jesus* has a biblical foundation and includes ready-to-implement counsel for ministries and classrooms. But the strength of this book is Marty and Deepak's conviction that God uses people—pastors, the children's minister, church members, and parents—to proclaim his glory to the next generation. This focus is why I'll be reading *Build on Jesus* with children's ministry leaders for many years."

Jared Kennedy, Managing Editor of *Gospel-Centered Family*; author of *The Beginner's Gospel Story Bible* and *Keeping Your Children's Ministry on Mission*

"What a great handbook for children's ministry! *Build on Jesus* is practical, spiritual, and an easy read. The authors give clear guidance for creating a ministry that is effective, sensible, safe, and fun. This book will be a great resource to those new to children's ministry and a great checkup for veteran children's ministers."

Annette Safstrom, Coauthor of *Sustainable Children's Ministry*; senior consultant, Ministry Architects

BUILD ON JESUS

A Comprehensive Guide to Gospel-Based Children's Ministry

Deepak Reju & Marty Machowski

newgrowthpress.com

New Growth Press, Greensboro, NC 27401
newgrowthpress.com

Where it is helpful and appropriate, names and details have been changed to protect the identity and confidentiality of people in the stories.

Cover Design: Faceout Books, faceoutstudio.com
Interior Design and Typesetting: Gretchen Logterman

ISBN: 978-1-64507-083-2 (Print)
ISBN: 978-1-64507-093-1 (eBook)

Library of Congress Cataloging-in-Publication Data
Names: Reju, Deepak, 1969- author. | Machowski, Martin, 1963- author.
Title: Build on Jesus : a comprehensive guide to gospel-based children's ministry / by Deepak Reju & Marty Machowski.
Description: Greensboro, NC : New Growth Press, [2021] | Includes bibliographical references and index. | Summary: "Build on Jesus equips ministry leaders with the right priorities, people, and practicalities needed for fruitful nurturing and care of the youngest disciples in the church"-- Provided by publisher.
Identifiers: LCCN 2021024175 (print) | LCCN 2021024176 (ebook) | ISBN 9781645070832 (print) | ISBN 9781645070931 (ebook)
Subjects: LCSH: Church work with children.
Classification: LCC BV639.C4 R449 2021 (print) | LCC BV639.C4 (ebook) | DDC 259/.22--dc23
LC record available at https://lccn.loc.gov/2021024175
LC ebook record available at https://lccn.loc.gov/2021024176

Printed in the United States of America

28 27 26 25 24 23 22 21 1 2 3 4 5

Contents

Introduction

Your Children's Ministry—Porsche or Junkyard Truck?

Picture a sunny day, and you're standing roadside, next to a racecourse. A 2020 Porsche 911 Carerra zips by you, moving at one hundred and eighty miles per hour. It's fast, sleek, and built for speed. Then, about fifty-three minutes later, here comes the competition—a 1977 Ford F-150, puttering along at twenty miles per hour. It's chugging along, with plenty of smoke coming out of the exhaust pipe. It looks like it's limping along. Your son whispers in your ear: "The F-150 is a classic!" but with the paint worn out and the frame bent out of shape, you're wondering if it belongs in the junkyard.

Is your church's children's ministry a Porsche or a junkyard car? Let's lift the hood and take a look at what's underneath.

A Typical Sunday—How Does It Look?

You stroll through your children's ministry wing at church on Sunday morning. You see smiling volunteers and colorful classrooms. Children and parents are moving everywhere, back and forth. Everything looks like it's running smoothly, maybe even like a fine-tuned Porsche engine that purrs like a kitten.

If you get under the hood, however, what you'll find is an old, beat up 1977 engine, barely alive. If you stood in the place of your children's ministry deacon or lead volunteer (or whoever oversees the kids in your church), what you'll see from *their* perspective is that problems abound.

- It's ten minutes before worship service begins. Cecelia just texted, "I'm horribly sick. I'm not going to make it in this morning." Where do you find a last-minute backup?
- Parents are standing outside of a classroom with their children, but none of the volunteers have shown up yet.
- An hour later, you walk by the kindergarten class. The smidgeon of volunteers is overwhelmed. There are a billion kids stuffed into the classroom (the first problem) and the volunteers clearly don't know what they are doing (the second problem).
- A teacher asks you, "Remind me what the bathroom policy is? I know you've told this to me before . . ." You get asked this question weekly by someone.
- A panicked mother grabs you after the service. "I saw a bruise on a one-year-old boy's leg. Should I call Child Protective Services? What should I do?"
- You're exhausted but survived the morning. You get home for a bite to eat and your traditional Sunday afternoon nap, but an irritated parent calls. "My son has got a cut on his arm. What happened in his class today?" No one told you about this, so you don't know what to say.

This sounds like the ministry is running much more like a junkyard Ford than a brand-new Porsche, right? The world of children's ministry, if you've ever served in it, is full of difficulties and frustrations. *Anyone* who has run a children's ministry can testify to it:

- There are not enough volunteers to keep the children's programs going.
- The volunteers that you do have are overworked and on the verge of burnout.

- You've never practiced an emergency evacuation and don't know what you'd do if there ever was a fire.
- There is pressure from church leadership to add additional programs, but they are reluctant to announce a need for more volunteers, unwilling to increase your budget, and they haven't set foot in children's ministry in years.
- There are reports about another church where the youth minister abused the teenagers. You think that couldn't happen here. But truth be told, if it happened in your church, you don't have the faintest idea how to handle it.
- Your curriculum is laden with moralistic lessons. You're fearful of creating little Pharisees in your children's programs. You want to change things up, but the teachers say, "We've always done it this way."
- A registered sex offender shows up at your church. You and your pastor don't know what to do.
- There are no clear check-in or check-out procedures, or no one follows the procedures you've put in place.
- Volunteers struggle to manage a rowdy crowd of children. There are more paper airplanes thrown around than Bible verses.
- You haven't been to a worship service in months and you're getting worn out. You'd love to attend regularly, but you constantly get stuck in the children's ministry, solving problems and filling in for last-minute dropouts.
- If something goes wrong (literally anything), you're winging it. There are no proactive plans or policies in place, or the policies you do have were written a decade ago and are no longer relevant.

That's not everything. We could fill up a few more pages with the problems that overrun children's ministry on a typical Sunday. If you are a children's ministry person, you think, *Yep. I've seen all of this. This is not new territory for me.* Or if you are the pastor, you think, *I knew there were problems, but I didn't realize all of what's gone wrong. That's a lot.* Or, if you are a parent, you might think, *Gosh, I had no idea*.

Is all of the time and effort put into children's ministry worth it? You're wondering what to do about these problems. What are effective ways to manage and get ahead of these challenges?

The Opportunity: Raise Up a Passionate Generation

Ten minutes. Ten children. Nothing to do. That's all it takes. Boredom is one of the great archenemies.

If you give a room full of children nothing to do, in a short while, they get rowdy and pick on one another, make paper airplanes, and find ways to get in trouble. The doctrine of depravity is foolproof (Romans 3:23). Children don't need to prove that they are sinners. Most kids by nature care more about themselves than God. Their short attention spans, their immaturity, and their nitpicking at each other all show that they are by nature foolish (Proverbs 22:15).

But with every challenge comes an opportunity. The vast majority of children waltzing around your church are not Christians. This means that by and large, the chance you have in every Sunday school class is to do more than teach a Bible story about David defeating the Philistine giant (though teaching Old Testament stories is good!). It's more than just providing safe childcare so the parents can attend the services undistracted (though that's a good thing to do!). It's more than singing gospel songs and memorizing Scripture (even more good stuff!). All of this is thinking far too small. What are you here for? Why are you laboring every Sunday morning for the sake of these kids? Stated simply, we organize children's ministry, recruit volunteers, and teach the Bible to these children because *our zeal is to see an entire generation of faithful believers raised up to proclaim the gospel to a world that needs it*.

That's right. This all starts in your class with a group of young children entrusted to you every Sunday morning. Are you up for the task?

Here's what we want to see. We want children who grow up to become Christians who stand firm when the cultural pressures contradict the Bible; boldly share the gospel with lost people; stand out as light to a dark world, a stark contrast to the self-glory, gluttony, and greed of this world; and willingly suffer and even die for the sake of Christ.

In short, we want another generation to carry the banner of gospel truth. How does this happen? Where does this new generation come from?

It comes from the Lord, of course. What we want—another generation of faithfulness—is what God has promised. He's told you that his Word will not fail (Isaiah 55:10–11), his kingdom has arrived and will go on (Matthew 4:17; 12:28; Revelation 11:15), he'll continue to draw sinners to himself (John 10:27–29), and—ready for this?—he'll use you to declare the saving work of Jesus to the upcoming generation who walks into your classroom.

Rest assured, you don't have to fix all of this mess on your own. Your job is to be faithful to teach, lead, and pray for the children, and God will do all the rest.

The Goal: Gathering—Both Now and Forever

You might say, "I can barely get the kids to pay attention, let alone cooperate. What you're asking for is a tall order." Well, we're not done yet.

Our more *immediate goal* is to see our children converted, growing up into believing adults who gather with the rest of the church. You want these children to know the Lord, and to be healthy, gospel-loving, servant-minded contributors to a local church. You can't save these kids; only God can (Jonah 2:9). But you are a means to point them to Christ and the cross. We share the gospel and pray that the Lord will convert their hearts and join them to our churches.

Our *ultimate goal* is to see our children one day gather with the great throng of believers—the thousands from every faithful generation—to worship the Lord in glory and enjoy him forever. We want to stand alongside these children—to sing, laugh, dance, embrace, and praise the greatness of our God.

Nothing short of these goals is worthy of your time or attention.

Your Map for the Road Ahead

Here's where we're headed.

Part 1 will cover the *priorities* of a children's ministry. We teach the Bible, and it's the foundation in everything we do. We think about children in the life of the church. What place do they have? What role do they play? We hold out the urgency of the mission—we instruct on the Great Commission as a worthy goal for their life.

Part 2 will deal with *people*. We want a hearty partnership between children's ministry and parents, pastors, and the congregation. If we sputter along like the junkyard Ford, the children's ministry director and a few volunteers will carry a thousand pounds of labor on a few people's backs. But, for this ministry venture to work well, all hands need to be on deck, lest this ship sink faster than the *Titanic*.

Part 3 will explain *practicalities*. We need best practices. How do we efficiently check in the children? How do we screen and train our volunteers? How do we design our children's ministry area to make it safe? We also need robust policies so we don't just react in the moment. What do we do if a fire takes place or an active shooter walks into the building? How do we respond to abuse and neglect? There are nuts and bolts to any children's ministry that need to be adequately dealt with to make it run smoothly.

If you are a children's ministry director—the main person who runs children's ministry in your church—we've composed this book for you. You're our target audience. There are no playbooks for your job, so we've compiled one for you. But we've also written with pastors in mind because they provide leadership to children's ministry and church members, especially the folks who volunteer day in and day out to keep it running. If you are a parent, reading this book will provide a guide for how to help improve your church's children's ministry. After all, you have a personal stake in the health of your church's ministry to the next generation.

God has entrusted to us the responsibility for these children. We desire nothing short of the best for our kids—a safe, well-run, creative, gospel-rich children's program that holds out the glories of Christ. If this is what you want too, then keep reading.

Part 1
The Priorities of Children's Ministry

We start by reviewing the priorities of children's ministry. Every ministry has priorities—the values, governing principles, and essential components foundational to our goals. We define and review these matters to help our ministry remain focused.

Take a minute and consider what values and principles define your ministry. What kind of foundation are you laying? What do your values reveal about your commitment to the gospel? Do your guiding principles show a commitment to the Bible? Do the leaders and adults in your church value children? How can you tell? What is the mission and how is it expressed?

Be aware that a church can run a successful children's program that everyone loves yet fall short of key priorities. We want to help our families reach the hearts of their children. When our kids reach their teen or young adult years, we hope they'll come to know and love the Lord personally, join the ministry, become members, and join the mission of our churches. We don't want our teenagers' beliefs to crumble and see them walk away from their faith.

Our foundation is key. We want our kids to stand on stable building blocks. These three priorities offer a rock-solid platform for any gospel-centered children's ministry:

Teach the Bible. The authority of the Bible and the gospel are the cornerstones on which we build our entire children's ministry. Everything we do is shaped and defined by these two values, including the gospel-rich curriculum we teach to our children.

Value the Children. Because Jesus valued children, so we also love and cherish them. That leads us to teach truth to little hearts and model the gospel in community for them.

Focus on the Mission. We want all of our kids to support the Great Commission and reach the world with the gospel, whether that's teaching a Sunday school class for thirty years in their local church or going overseas as a missionary.

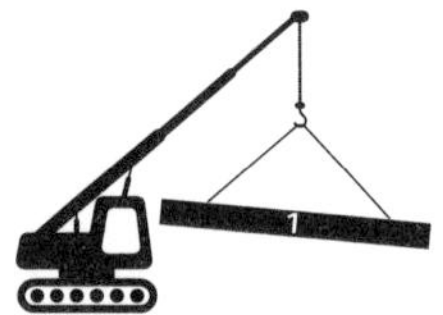

1. Teach the Bible

Peter, a thirty-year-old father of two preschool children, looks out at a room of seven six-year-olds. With eager anticipation, he stands tall on a chair and bellows with a loud voice, "I am the giant Goliath. Who here believes they are strong enough to fight me?" The children are instantly captivated by the dramatization, and several raise their hands to volunteer. The class follows along as Peter teaches them never to be afraid of the giants in their lives. The kids swing their imaginary slings with all their might and let their pretend stones fly. Then they watch as Peter falls in dramatic slow motion to the floor and then leads the class in a cheer. "We did it! We won! Thank you, God!"

The children return to their seats and color in their David and Goliath coloring sheets while Peter travels from table to table to help the class write their names on the upper right corner. The class is still abuzz as the parents come back to pick up their children.

"What did you learn about today?" Jennifer asks her six-year-old daughter, Kala.

Kala shouts her answer, "We beat the giant Goliath! We won, Mommy, we won!"

Peter quickly pipes in. "God helps us battle the giants. Doesn't he, Kala?" He makes sure Kala remembers that God is behind every victory.

Kala nods her head and takes her mom's hand. Jennifer leads her down the hallway and out the back door. She's grateful. "I'm so glad I started coming to this church. Peter is a great teacher."

Peter watches as the last of the kids exit the classroom. He is glad to teach, but he wonders how much of a lasting influence his lesson will have on the kids.

What's right or wrong with what Peter did here?

Are You Building on a Solid Foundation?

Just behind our house, I (Deepak) watched over the last year as construction workers built five three-floor, brick townhouses. Our family had a front-row seat to everything. Before they started building up, they dug down and set a solid foundation.

Before we answer the question about Peter ("What's right or wrong with what Peter did here?"), let's set out a few building blocks for your children's ministry—like the foundation for a building. Whatever you do stands atop some kind of foundation. When the tsunamis of life come blistering through, buildings with faulty foundations will crumble, like a toy house hit with a sledgehammer. Your building stands or falls based on the quality of your foundation.

Two crucial foundations stabilize our children's ministry: the authority of the Bible and the priority of the gospel.

First foundation: the authority of the Bible

The first foundation for your children's ministry—in fact, the cornerstone of the whole thing—is the authority of the Bible. 2 Timothy 3:16–17 reminds us, "All Scripture is breathed out by God and profitable for teaching, for reproof, for correction, and for training in righteousness, that the man of God may be complete, equipped for every good work."

The Bible is not just any book. It's the book of books. It's the norm of all norms. It's God-breathed. God is the author. The text was shaped, defined, and written by God, though the Lord used humans as a means for writing everything down. He's behind the men he inspired to write. The Bible has authority because God—who is the ultimate authority in this universe—wrote it. So, when the Bible speaks, God speaks. They are one and the same.

In light of this truth, we can draw out two implications.

1. Because the Bible is God's very own Word, it is trustworthy and true, without error.

We don't need a Thomas Jefferson Bible. The founding father used a razor and glue to cut and paste the parts of the Bible he liked. He got rid of all the parts he didn't like. The result was a Bible of his own making. Jefferson didn't believe in miracles (including the resurrection) so he literally cut them out.

Unlike Jefferson, we believe every book of the Bible is worthy of our children's attention because it is all from God. Though children gravitate to stories, let's not avoid using the Psalms, prophets, or New Testament epistles. Let's not create our own "Jefferson Bible"—cutting out the parts about sin and judgment or explaining away the miracles of Jesus. All Scripture is profitable for teaching!

2. Everything we do should be shaped by the Bible, because it's the very Word of God.

This second implication flows out of the first. If the Bible is written by God, then we should follow what it says. What God values, we should value. What God hates, we hate. His priorities should be our priorities. If God tells us to love him above all else, to serve others, to deny ourselves, to make sacrifices, then we show we trust him by following through with everything he commands.

The truth of Scripture should color all that we say and do in the classroom. When raw wool yarn is dyed, workers plunge the whole skein into the vat of dye. A sprinkle here and there is not sufficient. The goal is for the color to permeate every fiber. That is how we should use the Bible in our classroom. Scripture should shape what we teach, what we sing, the games we play, and the illustrations we use to present our lessons. Our kids are the wool that we plunge into the Bible vat of truth so that it soaks through to their heart and soul.

You want God's thoughts, God's words, and God's love to echo through all of your work.

Let's not allow our views, opinions, or philosophy of life to trump what the text of the Bible says. The Bible should be the heartbeat of your work.

We apply what the Bible says to our lives and allow it to shape how we live. If you allow the Bible to frame your teaching and permeate all that you do, you're building a rock-solid foundation for your ministry. Congratulations, that's a great way to start.

Second foundation: the gospel

The second cornerstone is the gospel. Gospel means "good news." It's God's good news of his one and only Son, Jesus Christ.

This gospel is the big picture theme of God's plan of salvation—it weaves its way through the whole Bible. Once you learn how to recognize it, you can see how every story connects to the larger gospel picture. The application of the gospel is the goal of every story. We want our children to know God personally through his Son, Jesus.

Consider the apostle Paul's words in 1 Corinthians 2:2: "For I decided to know nothing among you except Jesus Christ and him crucified." He tells the Corinthians that he didn't teach with lofty speech or all kinds of worldly wisdom (v. 1). The focus of his ministry was proclaiming Jesus's death on a cross on Calvary. In fact, all of Christianity can be summed up in four words: Christ died for sinners.

God's rescue plan can be summed up with just four words: GOD, MAN, CHRIST, and RESPONSE.

> GOD. God created men and women and put them in Eden, his perfect paradise (Genesis 1:26–28; 2:15).

MAN. Adam and Eve sinned. They rebelled against God and doubted his command (Genesis 3). They chose to trust the Satan's words rather than God's. Sin is our violation of God's law. All of mankind has turned its back on God; we have all declared we want to live life our own way (Isaiah 53:6).

CHRIST. God sent his only Son Jesus to redeem us. He took on the punishment we deserved, bore God's wrath, and then rose three days later as God declared him victorious over death itself (Mark 10:45; Romans 3:21–26; 6:9).

RESPONSE. What's required of all of us (including our kids) is to respond to this truth (John 1:12; Acts 17:30). We can't ignore or suppress it. We must decide if we'll give our life to Christ, as our Lord and Savior, or if we'll reject him.

We teach God's plan of salvation to our kids. The stakes are high. If we water down the gospel or replace it with a moral lesson, we deprive our children of God's true power. The apostle Paul said the gospel "is the power of God for salvation to everyone who believes" (Romans 1:16). Our salvation is rooted in believing and trusting in the substitutionary death of Jesus—that is, that Jesus absorbed God's wrath against our sin on the cross. Take that out of a Bible lesson, and you strip God's power from the story and leave your children empty. There are plenty of people who go to church, try to follow the Ten Commandments, and do good deeds but who are not trusting in Christ for their salvation. They remain lost.

It is through the gospel that our children come to know God and come to find joy, peace, and contentment that transcends their circumstances. This is how our living hope is passed down to the next generation. Because the gospel alone has the power of God to save, it is the key to ensuring our kids will one day be with God in heaven and join us in our mission to reach the lost (otherwise, they'll spend eternity in hell apart from the Lord).

We *must* teach the gospel. We don't have a choice. Eternity hangs in the balance.

Let's now answer our original question: What's right or wrong with what Peter did in the opening lesson at the beginning of this chapter? Peter certainly gave his all in his Goliath impersonation. Clearly, Peter cares about the kids in his classroom. But Peter missed the gospel in his retelling of the story. He took the famous story about David and Goliath and made it about underdogs beating the champions. The little guy beats the big, bad giant. We are to face the "Goliaths" of our day—whatever is big and scary in our life, whether that's a bully at school or a sickness at home.

Was that really the point of this story from 1 Samuel 17? In our evaluation, Peter's lesson is no better than generic proverbial advice you get from a fortune cookie or a high school coach in the locker room ("I know we've got a losing record, but we can beat the reigning champs!"). When Peter looked up from his script and gave the kids his own personal interpretation of the story, he turned it into a modern-day moral lesson about beating the big, bad things in your life—bullies, sickness, or the like. He got it wrong.

A careful look at 1 Samuel 17 shows what the point of the story is—in our weakness, we must fight to preserve the Lord's honor in all things.

1. Goliath defies the armies of the living God (vv. 26, 36). As sinners, we often do the same; we defy God and his ways.
2. David shows us what faith looks like—what trust in God is, even when the circumstances are bleak (vv. 46–47). God's past deliverance is the basis of our hope that he will continue to preserve us (v. 37).
3. David's weakness shows off God's strength (vv. 28–40). Despite how David's older brother Eliab (v. 28) and

Saul look down on David (v. 33), David's trust was in the Lord (v. 37). Saul tried to compensate for David's smaller size or strength (compared to Goliath) by giving David his own armor (vv. 38–39).

4. David is not the hero of the story. God is. God is the great deliverer of Israel. David's hope is in the Lord, not his own strength. So also, it is in God that we must put our hope. This story is not about little guys beating big, bad giants. It's about God, who will deliver the giant into David's hands ("This day the LORD will deliver you into my hands," v. 46).
5. David foreshadows Jesus. Goliath asks for a representative to stand for all of Israel. Not a single Israelite trusts God. They stand on the sidelines, afraid to fight. They need God to provide a savior, and God provides young David. When retelling the story, we shouldn't compare ourselves to David. We should compare ourselves to the sinful Israelites who needed a rescue. Jesus came, born in the city of David, in the kingly line of David, as one man who would represent sinners (that's all of us) and win the battle over sin and death (Romans 5:15). Everyone who puts their hope and trust in Jesus shares in Christ's victory and will live forever in heaven with God.

If one of your teachers taught 1 Samuel 17 next Sunday in your children's ministry, what would they say? Would they teach a moral lesson or connect the story with gospel truth? What would be the main points they communicate about this text? Here's our challenge to you: assign this text to one of your teachers and see what happens. It might be instructive.

Self-Evaluation: Are you building on a solid foundation?

What are the foundations for your ministry? What would people say is most important in your program? If you are not sure, a simple way to figure this out is to ask the senior pastor and a few parents whose kids attend your children's ministry. Are you building your children's ministry on these two solid foundations—the Bible and the gospel?

How to Assess Your Curriculum

With two solid foundations of your building in place, we can now pick out a curriculum to help you fulfill these scriptural, gospel-driven goals. As children's ministry leaders, we show our true colors by what we pick for our curriculum. We live and die by our curriculum choices because it shapes everything our teachers present to our kids. It's what our teachers teach and what our children consume. In whatever you pick, you communicate your priorities, hopes, and burdens for your children's ministry.

Most churches don't have time or energy to write their own curriculum. You buy prepackaged material—a curriculum in a box. What makes for a good curriculum? How do you evaluate it? What benchmarks do you use to pick out a curriculum that fits with your church?

Let us offer four criteria.

1. Content: Is it biblical and gospel-rich?

As you might expect, we want a curriculum that's rooted in the Bible and infused with the gospel. It should teach what the Bible says, so we can let God speak to our children. And it should regularly refer to the gospel because we desire our kids to hear the good news every time we gather. Do the children get the gospel in every lesson?

The gospel provides our main content. That's what we want woven throughout each lesson. If the lessons just teach good morals ("Be nice to old people." "Don't fight with your brother or sister." "The little guys can beat the champions if they work hard!"), then our children will never be saved. Our Sunday school will produce little Pharisees—religious people who know the rules but don't know Jesus. Is that what we really want?

2. Developmentally appropriate: Does it match a child's learning level?

I (Deepak) noticed my six-year-old son, Abraham, fidgeting. He squirmed in his seat and then blurted out, "I don't want to go to Sunday school." This surprised my wife and me. Our son has never been reluctant to go to church, so we were thrown off by his comment. My dear wife offered to sit in the class with him, and he reluctantly agreed to try again.

After church, I asked, "How did it go?" The response on her face communicated a lot (after twenty years of marriage, you don't have to exchange words to know if something is wrong). Here's what happened. There were two teachers, Zachary and Adeline. Adeline was crowd control—she was responsible for keeping the kids in line. Zachary "taught." He read from a script, with no enthusiasm in his voice, using big words like "atonement" and "justification." We're not opposed to teaching young children theological terms. But too many big words will zoom over the kids' heads faster than an F-15 fighter jet. My son didn't want to go back because he was confused and bored.

Your curriculum needs to be suited for where the children are—it should line up with what they can do cognitively, emotionally, and spiritually. Peter can tell a six-year-old, "Jesus atoned for your sins and propitiated God's wrath" or "Jesus died for you." The former is theologically accurate, but it's just too much for a first-grade boy or girl.

3. User-friendly: Is it easy to use?

You could tell by the creases in her forehead, the grimace, and her tightened facial muscles. Patricia looked like a deer in headlights. She had just picked up a copy of the Sunday school curriculum and was quickly overwhelmed. There were too many instruction pages, and there was so much material, she didn't know what to do. She was discouraged before she'd even started.

Curriculum should be easy to use and never overwhelming. If you've ever built something from IKEA, you know that they make the instructions as basic as possible. Otherwise, people like us would need to hire someone to build the furniture. If the instructions and curriculum aren't clear—if they are too cumbersome or confusing—the teacher will be discouraged. That's a problem. You want a curriculum that's user-friendly—easy to use and understand. That helps make the volunteer's preparation more efficient and enjoyable, and it removes barriers to communicating God's truth to children.

4. Fun and creative: Does it keep the kids engaged?

If we put seven six-year-old boys in a room for an hour with no toys, no lesson, and nothing to do, we're not sure they'll all make it out alive by the end of the hour. We're kidding (sort of). Kids get in trouble when they don't have anything to do. The last thing we need is more trouble in children's ministry.

Curriculum should be fun and engaging for the kids. If you throw truth at them, but your only target is their minds, the kids will struggle in class. The Puritan John Bunyan talked about the different gates to the heart—like the eye, ear, mouth, and nose gates.[1] A good curriculum will make use of these different senses and engage all of them.

I (Marty) recently taught the parable of the Pharisee and the tax collector (Luke 18:9–14). I wanted to help kids connect with the big idea—*it's not important what we are like on the outside, but what we are like on the inside*. So, I purchased two apples: one large, top shelf apple with a sticker, and one small, ordinary apple. The large apple was my Pharisee, and the small one my tax collector. Prior to class, I hollowed out the large apple from the bottom and stuffed it full of dried prunes. Then I used the two apples as props to tell the story.

I connected the New Testament story to the principal God taught Samuel, "[M]an looks on the outward appearance, but the Lord looks at the heart" (1 Samuel 16:7). As I spoke these words, I cut through the large apple with a knife, revealing the rotten core (the prunes). The children reacted predictably. Then

I told them. "The Pharisee trusted in his good works, but inside he was full of sin."

Then I cut through the middle of the smaller apple, revealing the star pattern formed by the seeds radiating out from the core. As I showed the children the star inside, I said, "The tax collector knew he was a sinner and asked God to forgive him. When we trust in Jesus who died on the cross in our place, God takes our sinful heart away. Instead of a rotten core, the tax collector had the Morning Star, Jesus, in his heart."

The kids didn't leave the classroom confused by Jesus's conclusion, "I tell you this man went down to his house justified, rather than the other" (Luke 18:14). The kids knew exactly what they needed: God must change their rotten heart of sin and the Morning Star (Jesus) must come to live in them. I'm sure at least some remembered God's words to Samuel, that God looks at the heart.

That's the big idea for the parable of the Pharisee and tax collector. But to be well rounded, engaging, and memorable, you can add more—a song, a craft, a skit, and even a snack—but let each and every activity reflect some aspect of that truth. Like the different sides of a diamond, we view this same truth through many different lenses.

You can sing a song about God changing our hearts. Have the children draw the two apples, one with a star and one with a rotten core, and even eat apples as a snack, to help the children remember the object lesson (always keep allergies in mind, though fresh fruit is one of the safest choices). You can have two children act out the proud words of the Pharisee in contrast to the humble tax collector. All together, these fun components work to underscore the gospel.

How Young Can You Start with Gospel-Rich Curriculum?

We start teaching gospel-rich content to young children—classes for two- or three-year-olds. Volunteers are often surprised by this. We've had teachers ask, "Are we really making a difference with children who can barely pay attention for more than two minutes?"

Yes, you're making a difference—in at least four ways.

1. *A young child's intake and processing of information is greater than his or her capacity to interact verbally.* At two years of age, a child can only speak fifty to two hundred words. But there is a lot more rolling around in the young child's head than can be expressed by his limited vocabulary.
2. *Repetition aids retention.* Have you ever had a young child ask you to read a favorite story for the twentieth time? A child can take in the same material over and over and over again because they enjoy it. We might only teach two-year-old kids a few minutes at a time because of their short attention span. But when you repeat the material, it greatly helps the child to retain and remember what he repeated.
3. *Children are sponges.* They absorb and learn from most everything around them. Adults tend to underestimate what little children can pick up.
4. *It is important to teach children ahead of their ability to understand.* Let's give them the gospel before they fully understand it. In this way, once they're able to understand, they'll have the gospel. Think of it in terms of building blocks. You can't build higher levels (of thinking) without laying down foundational layers. If we lay down a rock-solid, stable foundation, we can build more later on.

These kids learn more than they let on. For those who aren't quite ready to comprehend, let's share the good news about Jesus anyway. That way, as soon as they can understand, they'll have a foundation that will help them know Christ.

This Matters

It's Sunday morning at 9:30 a.m. Jake and Susan arrive at church with a quiver full of kids at hand and head to the children's ministry area. Jake pauses for coffee in the lobby and chats with a few other adults. Susan follows her kids as they race to the children's area. After she checks in their kids, Charlotte, their daughter, enters into her first-grade class.

Here's what we want her to encounter:

- Warm, kind, and gracious teachers. ("Good morning, Charlotte. I'm so glad to see you!")
- A solid Bible-based, gospel-centered curriculum.
- Fun, engaging, developmentally appropriate lessons.
- A welcoming and inviting environment.

What Peter teaches in his Sunday school class matters. We don't trivialize or minimize what he's doing. We help Peter get the lesson right so that Charlotte and the other kids can hear the gospel—the one truth that can change their lives. Through Peter's teaching, the Holy Spirit can bring conviction in the hearts of these little children, moving them from the domain of darkness to God's kingdom. Moral lessons won't suffice. We need them to walk away with more than just "The little guy beats the champions!" We need gospel-rich, Bible-saturated, developmentally appropriate, and creative truth that engages hearts, transforms minds, and changes lives. Glory be to God.

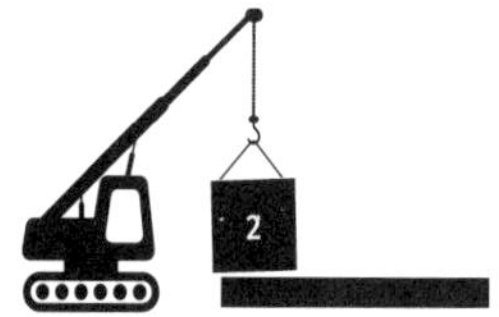

2. Value the Children

I (Deepak) was visiting a small church plant in a neighboring city. The senior pastor, Derek, was a godly man who faithfully taught God's Word every Sunday. He kindly asked me to fill in for him while he took some time away.

As a part of my visit, I asked Patricia, the children's ministry director, if I could get a tour of their facilities and learn about what their church does with the children. It's always instructive for me, and I learn something new every time I take a tour.

As Patricia walked me through the children's ministry section, we spoke about teachers, curriculum, check-in procedures, policies, and a whole host of other things. It was delightful to see her faithfulness, diligence, and commitment to what she does.

There was one noticeable problem, though. I observed several Sunday school classes, and they didn't have enough volunteers to staff their needs—an all-too-common challenge in children's ministry. I asked, "Why don't you or your pastor ask for more volunteers in the morning service?"

She looked squeamish for a moment. "I rarely meet with Derek. The one time I asked about recruiting at the worship services, he said, 'No.' He stated I just need to figure it out."

I wasn't surprised. Some of the godliest leaders I know believe children's ministry is a necessity to provide but not so much a responsibility of the pastors. Church leaders want children's programing—childcare, Sunday school, and children's church. Pastors know that if they don't have anything for the children, families won't come. But sadly, these same leaders don't want to be bothered with the details about the children's programs. They see it as a ministry to delegate. They recruit or hire a children's ministry director with a vision for kids. Then they leave it to the children's ministry director "to figure it out." At best, they touch base occasionally to see how things are going.

Let's put the most gracious possible spin on this situation—it's not that Derek doesn't value children or that he doesn't care for Patricia, the children's director. The problem is, like most pastors, Derek is overrun, overwhelmed, and pulled in every direction. When a pastor is stretched beyond his limits, children's ministry naturally drifts to the bottom of the pile of priorities. So as long as the children's programs are safe and the parents are not complaining, an overloaded pastor will put his attention elsewhere.

That leaves the children's ministry director and volunteers on a lonely island by themselves. They're stranded, without pastoral leadership, and left to make critical choices on their own.

Jesus Loves the Little Children

What does Jesus think? Our Lord came to save sinners—that includes adults, but what about the little children? Let's take a look at Mark 10:13–16:

> And they were bringing children to him that he might touch them, and the disciples rebuked them. But when Jesus saw it, he was indignant and said to them, "Let the children come to me; do not hinder them, for to such belongs the kingdom of God. Truly, I say to you, whoever does not receive the kingdom of God like a child shall not enter it." And he took them in his arms and blessed them, laying his hands on them.

The people were bringing children to Jesus. He was the great miracle worker, and many wondered if he might be the long-awaited Messiah.

The disciples rebuked the people who brought little children to Jesus. Children were the lowliest in their society—not valued and treasured. The disciples knew their master had much more important matters to attend to. Why bother him with these little children?

But the text says Jesus was indignant and displeased with his disciples. He didn't want the children sent away. Christ welcomed them. He loved them, and he extended a warm invitation: "Let the children come to me; do not hinder them."

And here is his reason: "for to such belongs the kingdom of God." God's kingdom was not a *physical* kingdom. It was the coming reign of Christ, where he was Lord, and as such, anyone who trusted Christ became a part of his kingdom. But how do children become a part of Christ's spiritual kingdom? They "receive" the kingdom—that is, they receive, welcome, and love Jesus, their King. The gospel is simple enough that even a child can understand and commit to it. God can redeem anyone, including the littlest of children.

Jesus warns in verse 15, "Truly, I say to you, whoever does not receive the kingdom of God like a child shall not enter it." Just as a little child can receive Jesus and come to him, so also, we should follow a child's example. We should receive Jesus as King—or else, we will not enter his kingdom.

Valuing and Welcoming Little Children Is Essential

Kristin had given birth to their first child, Rose. Bobby, the dad, was beaming about his newborn daughter. As they arrived at their apartment for the first time, Bobby walked Rose around to every room, introducing her to each part of the house. "This is mommy and daddy's bedroom . . . and this is the kitchen, where mommy and I will make your meals . . . and this is your nursery, where you will sleep . . ."

It was a precious sight—a father doting over his baby daughter. You might think, *She's just a baby. She doesn't understand what he's saying. That's just silly.* We'd say—no, in fact, it's not silly. Baby Rose is made in God's image and his likeness (Genesis 1:26–28). She, even as a baby, reflects the beauty of her Creator. As such, she deserves kindness, dignity, and respect.

Children are valuable to God. Scripture teaches us that children are to be sought after and celebrated (Genesis 33:5b; Psalm 127:3). As such, we should cherish and value them, just as the young father above built an atmosphere of love and welcome for his baby daughter.

I (Marty) remember talking to a church planter who worked out a deal to meet in a large, stone church building. The original church's congregation had dwindled to a few dozen folks, all in their seventies and eighties. This local church was dying. Why? They lost the next generation. Fortunately, the older congregation recognized their problem and welcomed the church plant to take over their facility. The older folks happily joined the church plant, and almost instantly, a vibrancy of church life was restored to them.

We need to keep the next generation central to the ongoing mission of the church.

Amid the destruction of the previous nine plagues and with the threat of another, Pharaoh relented and offered to allow Moses to leave Egypt with the men but to leave the "little ones" behind (Exodus 10:7–11). Pharaoh understood the importance of the children. But so did Moses, who refused to leave the little ones behind. "We will go with our sons and our daughters," he insisted. When Pharaoh refused, Moses stretched out his hand and brought a plague of locusts upon Egypt, the likes of which had never been seen.

We must build our churches with the same vision for the importance of the next generation, just like Moses. How vital were these children to Israel's future? This generation of Israelite children made it into the promised land when their doubting, unbelieving parents were refused entry by God.

Where Do Our Children Fit into a Local Church?

Scripture describes a local church as a spiritual family (John 1:12–13; Romans 8:14–17; Galatians 3:26; Ephesians 1:5). God is our Father, and he adopts us into his family. In fact, we refer to fellow church members as brothers and sisters, fathers and mothers, to reflect this spiritual reality. We gather on Sundays, worshipping together and building community with one another.

From the beginning, we integrate children into the family life of our church. We pursue this through two big goals: (1) teach truth to little hearts, and (2) model gospel community. Both goals help our kids become a vital part of a local church. The things we do for our biological children we extend to all the children within our local church community.

Teach truth to little hearts

In Psalm 78, the Lord speaks, "Give ear, O my people, to my teaching; incline your ears to the words of my mouth!" (v. 1). God invites his people to listen to his teaching and join him in reaching the next generation. Imagine all of Israel singing: "We will not hide them from their children, but tell to the coming generation the glorious deeds of the Lord, and his might, and the wonders that he has done" (v. 4). We are not to hoard the truth to ourselves, but we are to share it with the coming generation.

The "we" in verse 4 is not just parents. While parents have the primary responsibility to instruct their children, it doesn't fall exclusively on their shoulders. This psalm addresses *all* believers. Telling of the glorious deeds of the Lord is a community project, something all of us are called to do. Thus, church members have a responsibility to tell truth to their children.

Ken was volunteering as a hall monitor on Sunday morning. He noticed that a young boy, Timothy, was upset on his way back to his class from the restroom. Ken talked with Timothy, comforted him, and most importantly, reminded this young child of truth. That afternoon, Ken was more than just a hall monitor. He was a truth-teller, comforter, and communicator of the gospel to this little kid.

That's how the church should work—it's not just parents, but every adult who walks in the doors of the church building, every adult who talks to a kid after church, every volunteer in childcare, every Sunday school teacher, every hall monitor—each and every one has an opportunity to communicate the glories of our great God to these children. You don't have to be in a more formal role, like a preacher or a Sunday school teacher, to be a conveyer of truth to church kids.

The hope and prayer is that one generation will tell of the Lord to the next generation, and that generation will tell the next, and that generation will tell that next, and so on, such that

> they should set their hope in God
> and not forget the works of God,
> but keep his commandments;
> and that they should not be like their fathers,
> a stubborn and rebellious generation,
> a generation whose heart was not steadfast,
> whose spirit was not faithful to God. (Psalm 78:7–8)

We don't want God to be forgotten. We don't want to end up as a group of seventy-year-olds who've lost our kids. We must stand with the same tenacity Moses demonstrated to Pharoah and declare, "We will not go without our children!" Like Asaph in Psalm 78, we teach children and model our faith before them because we want them to set their hope in God—who is the greatest and best hope they could ever have. And we also hope to prevent our children from being like the stubborn and rebellious generation who rejected God.

Self-Evaluation: Teach truth to little hearts

How is your teaching ministry doing? Are the Sunday school teachers and children's church volunteers faithfully communicating the truth of God's Word? Or do they just share their own personal opinions and general thoughts about life? What about the childcare workers, hall monitors, and other roles in your ministry—do they also work to teach truth to the kids? Do they seize the unexpected opportunities that God provides? Are your volunteers committed to loving the children and living together as a church family? Does the responsibility to teach the next generation fall on just a few folks, or do a lot of church members see teaching children as a priority?

Model gospel community

Every parent needs allies, since parenting is difficult work. It's joyous and rewarding, but it's also challenging. Families need more than just parents speaking into their kids' lives.

That's where parenting in a community makes an immense difference. The burden shouldn't just fall on a parent's shoulders. The apostle Paul frequently talks about modeling gospel living in community. He encouraged fellow believers, "Be imitators of me, as I am of Christ" (1 Corinthians 11:1) and "Keep your eyes on those who walk according to the example you have in us" (Philippians 3:17). Just like Paul, believers are called to be examples to one another and the children in our church. Children are watching the adults around them. When our kids see other believers teach the same truth and model the same practices, it affirms the core beliefs taught and modeled at home. To a child, observing a Christian adult is like watching the gospel turned into a movie—kids see Christianity in action in all kinds of ways.

In many churches, the singles hang out with the singles, and the married folks spend time with the married folks. Rarely do the two fellowship together, apart from families asking singles to babysit. But what if we tore down the dividing wall? What if teenagers, singles, couples without kids, parents with kids, empty nesters, and seniors regularly engaged one another? What if it was normal for them to do more than just talk to each other briefly after Sunday services, but to do life together?

What if other adults in the church (not just Sunday school teachers) helped in the discipling of our children? What if we regularly welcomed singles and couples and seniors over for dinner, so that our kids could build relationships with them? What if my (Marty's) small-group leader also coached my son or daughter in soccer? Or my (Deepak's) wife invited two single women from our church to go on vacation with our family? What if there was so much cross-pollination—so many overlapping relationships with a family—that our kids couldn't help but run into the gospel each and every day? They would see a genuine example of gospel life (with all its joys and trials) lived out in the lives of our church members.

There are church members who are engaged daily, weekly, and even monthly with our families. And most of what we're describing doesn't occur within the church building—we're not talking about the formal children's programs offered at the church. Every example we mentioned (one-on-one discipling, having members over for dinner, singles joining us for vacation) shows how church members can engage families (parents and children alike) *outside* of the public worship services.

A lot of evangelical churches rightly emphasize the importance of preaching God's Word and teaching sound doctrine. But what many churches lack is a clear sense of community. A compelling, supernatural community can be a vital witness to our kids because it models gospel living. Fellow church members display the gospel every day in the little daily interactions with our families. If we put this responsibility solely on the shoulders of our Sunday school teachers or youth minister, we show that we don't get what it means to be a community together. It takes an *entire* church to raise a family.

Self-Evaluation: Model gospel community

As you look at your church, do you see a supernatural community where people are investing in each other's lives? Are people willing to make sacrifices and give up daily comforts to be engaged with one another? What would it take to build a gospel community that models Christian living to our children? Do our kids see the gospel lived out faithfully? If not, it is easy to get such a community started. Begin by inviting a godly single over for a meal and invite them to share what God is doing in their life. It is as simple as that.

Precious in His Sight—and Ours

Look across your congregation on a Sunday and guess at how many children and teens were converted while at home. What's your guess? Ten percent? Twenty percent? Fifty percent?

A few months ago in my (Deepak's) church, Pastor Mark stated, "If you think you were converted by the time you were three, please stand up." A few people in the congregation stood up. Then Mark added, "If you think you were converted by four, please stand." A moment later, ". . . by five, please stand." And he went on, ". . . by six, please stand . . . by seven . . . by eight. . ."

When Mark got to age seventeen, about 75 percent of the church was standing. He went on to make his point. "Look at how many people were converted during their years in children's or youth ministry. It was most of our church! Let's remember, and not take for granted, how important our work is with the children. God can save these children, and he can use you to bring the gospel to bear on their lives."

Children are precious to Jesus. And they are also to us, so we should do everything we can to make them a valuable part of our churches.

3. Focus on the Mission

Leo's mom hung on to him while she tried listening to the service through a speaker mounted in the lobby. Leo's too-big-to-be-a-three-year-old body struggled to break free from his mother's desperate grip.

I knew Leo should be in class, but he wasn't. About an hour earlier, his teacher had posted his parents' number on the sanctuary monitor because of Leo's attitude and behavior yet again. *That kid is trouble*, I thought. *How are we ever going to reach him?*

At that moment, I lost sight of the big picture and looked instead to the obstacles. Have you ever wondered how you would raise up another generation who would carry on the mission? I could have used a Joshua-style pep talk to reset my focus, the kind he received from the Commander of the Lord's army just before launching into the promised land: "Be strong and courageous. Do not be frightened, and do not be dismayed, for the LORD your God is with you wherever you go" (Joshua 1:9). Today the mission of the Commander of the Lord's army is clear. Jesus said, "I will build my church, and the gates of hell shall not prevail against it" (Matthew 16:18). As children's ministry workers, it is our job to join with parents to see this mission passed on to the next generation. Just before returning to be with the Father, Jesus charged his disciples (and now us) with carrying on his mission. Note how he repeated the promise made to Joshua—the promise to never leave us to do it alone: "Go therefore and make disciples of all nations, baptizing them in the name of the Father and of the Son and of the Holy Spirit, teaching them to observe all that I have commanded you. And behold, I am with you always, to the end of the age" (Matthew 28:19–20).

Here are a few key questions: What does it take to raise a generation of children who will carry on with the mission of the church after us? How do we get kids who forgo personal comforts to serve at our local churches, make intentional sacrifices to be a part of a church plant, or even leave all behind to take the gospel overseas? What's it going to take to reach the Leos in our ministries and empower them to faithfully serve the Lord?

How Do We Help Our Children Develop a Passion for the Mission?

Let's examine five elements that help our children develop a passion for service to the Lord: model, teach, expand, expose, and pray. We'll explain each one in turn.

1. Model

The apostle Paul understood that mission is better "caught" than "taught." Paul's message to believers was not so much, "Do what I say," but rather, "Follow my example and imitate me" (1 Corinthians 4:16; Philippians 3:17; 4:9). Teaching *about* the mission of the local church and missions abroad are important, but not more important than modeling a love for the mission in our own lives. The unsaved and unreached children that visit our Sunday school classrooms, Awana clubs, or summer VBS may become our next pastors, church planters, or missionaries.

Nothing infuses a passion for reaching the world more than a teacher who demonstrates a hunger for Jesus and reaching the lost. Never underestimate the effect of a zealous teacher's life upon our students.

I (Marty) recently spoke to Leo, the troublemaker, who now serves as a pastor at our church! I asked him to think back on his children's ministry days and what influenced him. After a moment, he said he couldn't remember any one particular weekly lesson from his children's ministry days. But his voice filled with excitement as he recollected several children's ministry teachers and the influence their passion had on his impressionable life. Leo remembered Bauer's enthusiastic, Spirit-filled leading of worship. He recounted Jamie's fascinating object lessons and enthusiasm whenever he taught the kids. Leo talked about these teachers' influence, and the many verses of Scripture pressed into his heart and how the Spirit of God later used this rich deposit to reach him. After high school, Leo became a teacher in the inner city, where he modeled the same kind of teaching he learned from Jamie. He became a worship leader for our church and modeled the same Spirt-filled worship he learned from Bauer. Eventually, Leo received a call to pastoral ministry, and after his ministry schooling, joined a church plant we sent out to reach the multiethnic neighborhood he grew up in. That church, Risen Hope, soon filled its pews with people from more than a dozen different ethnicities, with Leo serving as an assistant pastor, leading worship.

After helping establish Risen Hope, Leo returned to our home church. Today, as one of our full-time elders, he serves in worship ministry, works with the youth, and leads our global initiatives ministry to reach the world with the gospel. Who would have guessed that a rambunctious toddler would end up in a job that proclaims and spreads the gospel?

Our efforts in the classroom can set our students' hearts ablaze with a desire to reach others with the gospel—from folks in their neighborhood to the unreached people groups of the world.

2. Teach

We teach our kids about their obligation to obey the Great Commission, the beauty of sacrifice, and the painful reality of persecution.

The obligation to go: At the end of Matthew's Gospel, Jesus proclaims the authority given to him by his Father. Not just *some* authority, but "*all* authority in heaven and on earth." He then tells his disciples to go make disciples of all nations (Matthew 28:18–20). His gospel is for all peoples of the earth, because he is Lord of all. His followers are to go, baptize, and teach.

What our Lord lays out in Matthew 28 is a command. There is an imperative force in what he says. He puts it as an obligation, not a suggestion. And it all starts with the simple verb "go." *Some* of our kids must obey Jesus and go to people and places outside our local area. *All* of our kids should be involved in this work with their time, money, and energy.

The beauty of a sacrificial life: After we teach our kids Christ's command to go, we also explain to them that there is beauty in a sacrificial life. Jesus gave up his place with his Father in heaven, to take on human flesh and become a servant (Philippians 2:5–7). He humbled himself to the point of death, even death on a cross (Philippians 2:8). Just as Jesus humbled himself, so also, in humility, we should put others ahead of ourselves (Philippians 2:3–4). Even though this is costly, we're willing to sacrifice our lives for others because of Christ.

In contrast to our selfish and self-exalting world, Christ laid down his life and calls us to do the same. Our hope is that our kids would one day be willing to give up their lives for others. The beauty of a sacrificial life is on display as we share the gospel with our unbelieving coworkers, leave our friends behind to participate in a church plant, or learn a new language and move abroad to translate the Bible for an unreached people group.

The painful reality of persecution: While there is real beauty in a sacrificial life, there is also pain and suffering. We need to be honest with our children about the hard things—including the world's hatred and persecution of Christ's disciples (John 17:14). We don't sell our church kids a Pollyanna view of the mission. No, we're honest about the toil and turmoil. There is suffering if you attach yourself to Jesus (Luke 6:22; John 15:18; Philippians 1:29; 2 Timothy 3:12). Christians are spit on, threatened, whipped, beaten, thrown in prison, and killed for the sake of Christ. Some lose their jobs and are socially ostracized. Our children need to know the painful realities of following Christ. We only hurt our kids if we hide the ugly parts of the Christian's calling.

Self-Evaluation: Teach

Do you, your teachers, and helpers demonstrate a passion for the mission before your kids? Do you teach the Great Commission from Matthew 28? Do you teach them about the beauty of sacrifice but also the reality of suffering as a Christian? Do you see the Leos of your church as trouble, or can you envision your kids as one day following Jesus to reach the world with the gospel?

Here's a practical way to measure this last point. Do a quick review of your curriculum. Does it offer a squeaky clean and sanitized view of the Christian life, or is it honest about a Christian's sacrifice and suffering?

3. Expand

We want to expand our kids' view of God. We don't want them to know a teeny-tiny god who is powerless and does nothing. We want them to know a *big God* who does great and glorious things and rules the world with all power and authority.

My (Deepak's) pastor prays weekly for God's work throughout the world. He offers general prayers: "God convert people," "change their hearts," "help us to know your love." But he also prays specifically for God's work in the lives of different rulers and nations of the world. I've heard him pray for God to convert a dictator and dethrone a king. "God, you hold the hearts of kings in your hands, we ask today that you would regenerate the heart of ______________. You can do this, Lord, and we ask this of you today." He prays big and bold prayers because he believes in a *big God* who can do anything, anywhere, at any time. His God is not small and limited. He's all-loving, all-powerful, all-knowing, and all-present.

Let's translate this into children's ministry work. If we hold out to our children a small view of God, it will lead our kids to have small thoughts, to not take risks, and to not do much with their lives. A small god does little in this world and asks little of us. But our big God changes hearts and rearranges this world for his glory. We want our kids to see this big God who runs the entire universe. Which God do you personally believe in? Which God are you holding out to your children?

4. Expose

Just as we expand our kids' view of who God is, so also we expose our children to a big world. We proactively open their eyes to the different languages, cultures, foods, dress, and histories from the corners of the globe. We share stories of those who are faithfully serving God in contexts different from our own.

Kids naturally have a small view of this world—they don't think beyond their neighborhood. We want our children to see beyond these limitations and entrust themselves to a big, creative God in a big world.

Picture this situation. Jonathan is in his thirties, tall and thin. He's a faithful member of his church, and after the morning worship service, he picks up his six-year-old son, Mark, from a children's class.

Jonathan stands just outside the doorway of his son's class, looking in. "Hey, son. Please say thank you to your teacher."

Little Mark turns his head to his teacher, Sally, and says, "Thank you." He turns back to his dad and holds out a coloring sheet with the outline of Uganda. Inside, two small stars mark the location of two villages. "Dad, look at what I colored!"

Jonathan leans in, smiles, and says, "Wow, Mark. What country did you learn about today?" Mark ponders his father's question for just a moment and replies, "We learned about Uganda and our missionaries who work there. We sang a Japadola song today! That's their language!"

In this small interchange, what we're offering is a glimpse into little Mark's world. Not only was he excited to show off his coloring sheet, but he displayed knowledge about a foreign country, missionaries who were serving there, and even a little bit about their culture. That might not seem much, but from the limited vantage point of a six-year-old, it's a step in the right direction. He's showing he can see beyond the limits of his life and neighborhood to the greatness of God's work in this fallen world.

Self-Evaluation: Expose

Do another spot check of your curriculum. Does it offer your children an expanding view of God's world and his work across the globe? Does it teach them about missionaries and their sacrifices for the gospel?

5. Pray

I (Deepak) am standing at the back door of our church after the morning worship service, where our pastor just preached an inspiring message on Romans 10.

> How then will they call on him in whom they have not believed? And how are they to believe in him of whom they have never heard? And how are they to hear without someone preaching? And how are they to preach unless they are sent? As it is written, "How beautiful are the feet of those who preach the good news!" (vv. 14–15)

Our pastor emphasized the words of verse 15, "unless they are sent." The missions imperative requires that some must *go* to bring the gospel to people who desperately need to hear it.

On her way out, I talked with Julie, a parent of four adorable children, and she was brutally honest with me. Her confession was something like this: "I don't want my kids to be missionaries. Don't get me wrong. I pray for and financially support our missionaries. Evangelizing the world is vital work. It's God's work. I pray often for the Lord to save my kids, but I love them so much I selfishly don't want to give them up. I can't stand the thought of sending them to a foreign country—where they could face persecution, hardships, and even death. I'm scared to give them up to God and risk losing them or rarely seeing them. Pastor, please pray for my heart."

What do you think? If parents were honest with you, is this what they'd tell you? Do you have a Julie in your congregation?

Matthew recounts, in his Gospel, this story about Jesus:

> And Jesus went throughout all the cities and villages, teaching in their synagogues and proclaiming the gospel of the kingdom and healing every disease and every affliction. When he saw the crowds, he had compassion for them, because they were harassed and helpless, like sheep without a shepherd. Then he said to his disciples, "The harvest is plentiful, but the laborers are few; therefore pray earnestly to the Lord of the harvest to send out laborers into his harvest." (Matthew 9:35–38)

Christ exhorts his disciples about the spiritual need of the harvest. There are many ready to receive the good news of his coming. So, he commands his disciples (and also us) to "pray earnestly." We participate in God's spiritual harvest by praying the Lord would raise up laborers for his harvest.

We pray that our kids would *go* and tell the good news. Their efforts to share the gospel starts with telling a younger sibling about Jesus. Later in life, as they grow, we want them to also take the gospel beyond the walls of their homes, into the world. We give over our hearts—and our children—to the Lord, as we seek to fulfill the Great Commission.

Practical Ideas to Make Your Children's Ministry More Focused on the Mission

Here are a few practical suggestions about how to make your children's ministry more mission focused. If these ideas aren't a fit for your church, develop ideas that would be better for your context.

Visualize God's work in his world

Put a map up of the world for your kids to see every week when they come to church. If it is appropriate and safe, mark off the location of any church plants your church has sent out and the countries the missionaries you support are serving in. Add photos if you have them. It's an excellent reminder for the kids that God's kingdom is bigger than your local church.

Talk about your mission

Talk about your efforts to reach your local neighborhoods with the gospel. Christmas and Easter provide great opportunities to invite neighbors. Our church (Marty) offers evangelistic opportunities for families on the second Sunday of the warmer months. Kids get involved with their parents washing cars and joining their parents for other initiatives like delivering gift bags to folks who visited our church over the past month. Get your kids excited about participating in gospel work, and they will take their parents with them!

When your church sends out a church plant or a family moves to join in one, your kids know. Often they have friends leaving with the church plant! Take time to talk about the different church plants and the joy of starting new gospel work.

Our mission is not just local. It also involves bringing the gospel to other countries and cultures. Share about overseas workers you support in other parts of the world. Even better, when missionaries are visiting stateside, have them talk with your kids. You want your children to hear about the obstacles to the gospel (e.g., cultural and religious barriers), the realities of the cost of following Christ (e.g., believers die for their faith), and the testimony of God's work in this world. Read missionary stories and commend biographies. Let the kids learn about Christians who sacrifice their life for the sake of the gospel. Ensure somewhere in your scope and sequence that you teach about the obligation to go and proclaim the gospel throughout the world. See if it is integrated throughout your classes and teach a specific class on overseas work and missionaries.

Display different cultures, tastes, sights, and sounds

As you build a curriculum that talks about overseas work, you can also help your children to see, taste, smell, and experience different parts of God's beautiful world.

Children play with different toys around the world. Ask a missionary from your church to bring back a toy that kids play within the country they serve. Use it to talk about the culture of the people you are trying to reach.

Foods from different cultures provide an opportunity to talk about countries where your church supports a missionary or church plant. The smells of curry filling the room can make your discussion about a missionary to India much more exciting.

Crafts can be fun for the kids. They might display the written language from the culture where a missionary serves. For example, find out how they spell "Jesus saves" and have the kids write that with markers on a river rock along with the reference 1 Peter 2:6.

Keep the End Goal in Mind

Humanly speaking, the church's future depends on the kids in our classrooms. These little ones one day will take up the mission and carry on from where we left off. Despite how bad they might be at times, don't write off the Leos of your children's ministry. They, as Leo did, may grow up to become pastors, members of a church plant, or missionaries overseas. It's hard to see this now, but trust that God can do more with Leo than you could ever imagine.

The mission to reach the world will continue until the day our Lord returns. Let's do all we can to equip our children to join in the mission of proclaiming Jesus near and far.

Part 2
The People in Children's Ministry

In part 1, we offered three priorities on which to build a firm, unshakable foundation for our children's ministry: Teach the Bible. Value the children. Focus on the mission. This is the right kind of foundation on which to build all the rest.

Now we'll shift gears. In part 2, we look for people. At the center of God's redemptive plan is a rescue operation—God uses fallen, broken sinners and sufferers (like you and me) to inspire, instruct, and model truth to little hearts.

God uses people to proclaim his glory. Who will lead the staff and volunteers? Who will teach and love the children? Who will organize and execute our children's program? Who are key players who make this all work? We need committed, Jesus-loving, Word-saturated people to run children's ministry.

Let's consider the people who keep the engine running and well maintained in children's ministry.

> **Pastors Lead and Shepherd.** Somebody needs to show leadership, cast a vision for reaching the next generation, care for the staff, set the priorities and limits, make key decisions, and provide momentum when things are slowing down. This and more belongs to pastors who oversee the children's ministry.

Children's Ministry Directors Organize and Execute. The staff are the hands and feet on the ground organizing and executing to make children's ministry happen. A key person makes sure children's ministry does what it is supposed to do. Programs are organized, volunteers are trained and in place, members are recruited, curriculum is chosen and distributed, and so on.

Members Maintain Children's Ministry. If the staff (and deacons) build the trellis, the members show up and do the work of growing the vine. They teach, instruct, and watch over the children. They keep the children's ministry going by their presence, energy, and loving efforts.

Parents Build a Robust Partnership. Parents entrust their children to the children's ministry team, who provide a safe and gospel-centered environment for the children. Likewise, the children's ministry team equips parents to be the primary disciplers of their children during the rest of the week. What's formed is a healthy gospel partnership between both sides.

4. Pastors Lead and Shepherd

I (Marty) can remember attending a local Christian school for a children and youth pastors' appreciation breakfast. I introduced myself to three pastors I had never met before. At the time, I had been pastoring at the same church around twenty years. Leading children's ministry was my main area of ministry, along with caring for small groups in our church.

When it came to my turn to answer the question, "So what do you do?" I replied, "I lead our children's ministry." I could tell what they were thinking, *This guy is in his early forties and he is still leading children's ministry?* Their follow-up question gave away their concern. "So how long have you been doing that?" When I answered twenty years, their heads dropped in unison, looking to the floor. I could tell they were thinking, *Poor chap; he's been doing this for two decades and he's not even been able to advance to youth ministry!* I didn't let their noticeable silence carry on. I shared my vision for reaching the next generation and vision for reaching our children to a chorus of head nods and meek smiles. I wanted them to know my excitement to lead in children's ministry—that working with children is more than a stepping-stone to something greater.

It's hard to fault pastors for not seeing the priority of children's ministry. Aspiring pastors don't get much, if any, instruction on children's ministry in seminary. They spend a year learning Greek and Hebrew, receive months of training on how to exegete the Bible, take a course or two about counseling and practical ministry, and perhaps one day hear a lecture that touches on children's ministry. I can remember getting invited to teach one of those "squeeze all a pastor needs to know about ministry to children into four hours" sessions to a group of future pastors. The class warmly welcomed me. They were grateful for the opportunity to sit back and relax and not have to worry about an exam. When I closed the day with a question-and-answer time, they all asked the same question: What is the best way to find a champion to whom they could delegate this task?

The goal of this chapter is to think through the pastor's role in children's ministry. Our contention is that regardless of the size of the church, there should be a pastor involved—the senior pastor or an associate pastor or even a lay pastor (if your church structure allows such a thing).

The Pastor's Connection to Children's Ministry

A pastor has both theological incentive and practical considerations as he figures out his relationship to children's ministry.

Theological incentive: shepherding God's flock

The pastor's responsibility for the care and instruction of his church's children is a vital part of his overall charge to shepherd God's flock. He can delegate the work, but he still remains responsible for the care of these children's souls. Pastors are called to be shepherds over both the adults and the children of their congregations.

In writing to Christians who were suffering for their faith, Peter says this to the elders:

> So I exhort the elders among you, as a fellow elder and a witness of the sufferings of Christ, as well as a partaker in the glory that is going to be revealed: *shepherd the flock of God that is among you, exercising oversight*, not under compulsion, but willingly, as God would have you; not

> for shameful gain, but eagerly; not domineering over those in your charge, but being examples to the flock. (1 Peter 5:1–3, emphasis added)

Just as a shepherd would tend to the flock, so also does a pastor. Do you know how to tell who a pastor is? You can tell because he's dirty and grimy, and he smells like his sheep. The basic job description of every pastor is to care for, protect, and guide God's sheep. That includes everyday church members, but among those members, the pastor has a special responsibility to lead and love the church staff.

A pastor shouldn't ignore children's ministry. He shouldn't leave his staff on their own to figure out how to organize and run the entire enterprise. Children's ministry leaders prosper when they're led by their pastor. If you are a pastor reading this and realize you've been falling short but don't know where to start, it is not complicated. The simplest and most effective action a pastor can take is to give some of his time. It's not rocket science—block time off in your schedule. Meet with, encourage, build into, and care for the children's ministry staff. Be consistent, available, thoughtful, a good listener, a problem solver, a sounding board for their ideas, humble, and gracious.

Practical considerations: sample organization charts

In most small churches, it's the senior pastor with a skeleton staff. The senior pastor who preaches every Sunday can't also direct the children's ministry program. That's too much for one person. More than likely he'll find a key volunteer who will take up the cause or pay someone to do this part-time.

In a small church, the children's ministry leader will report directly to the senior pastor. This is at times a difficult option because the senior pastor has so many demands on his time, without much help. It won't be easy to give time and attention to children's ministry, but God's grace the pastor can!

If the church has more than one pastor, like an associate pastor or a plurality of pastors/elders, a more realistic option is for any other pastor (aside from the senior pastor) to take responsibility for oversight of the children's ministry. The children's ministry director reports to the associate pastor for his or her daily work. That's more reasonable considering the burdens on a senior pastor's time.

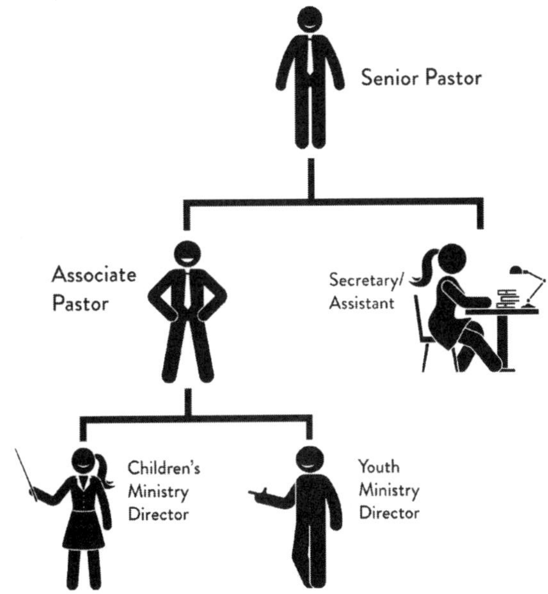

A pastor needs to take responsibility and oversee the children's ministry. If you were to ask your children's ministry director and volunteers who they report to, what would they say? Is it clear which pastor provides leadership for children's ministry?

The Qualities of a Pastor who Shepherds Children's Ministry

If the overarching charge on a pastor's life is to shepherd God's flock (including leading the children's ministry), then what next? What does the pastor do? How does he help? What hard things must he say? Where does he support, train, set limits, and advocate?

1. The pastor leads and loves

Leadership and love sit atop the pastor's job description. The pastor steers the ship. He's the captain, at the helm, in the middle of the storm, staring out on the deck and declaring, "Go this way, not that way." He's known as the leader for children's ministry, and he takes responsibility for it. He guides the staff, volunteers, and parents in a gospel-centered, God-glorifying direction. He provides teaching priorities and guidance for the programs and volunteers.

He also takes responsibility for failure. US President Harry Truman kept a sign on his desk that read, "The buck stops here." If someone abuses a child under your care or treats a child poorly in the classroom, if there is a fire but no evacuation plan, if the children's ministry staff are disorganized or experiencing conflict and no one is mediating, or if there are not enough volunteers, the pastor should step in, take responsibility, and bring caring oversight to the situation.

Pastors are never dictators; they are servant-leaders. Christ came "not to be served, but to serve, and to give his life as a ransom for many" (Mark 10:45). So also, his disciples (especially pastors!) should do the same. The pastor should have an evident love for those who work and serve in children's ministry.

2. The pastor sets out the big picture

I (Deepak) was sitting in my car, heading out to take my kids to soccer practice, and my daughter Lydia asked, "Why do you do that?" Every time we pull out of the parking lot, I switch the GPS from the street view (where you can just see the street right around you) to the overview page (where you can see the entire route to your destination). You're now wondering, *Why does he do that?* Because I want to see the big picture—to anticipate obstacles and figure out what it takes to get to our destination.

The pastor needs to know enough details to understand how things run in children's ministry and have a good feel for what works and doesn't work. But he also needs to step back and see the big picture—how it all fits together and where it's headed.

The pastor leads the children's ministry team by providing a view of the bigger picture. He guides them throughout their journey. He sets out the priorities and values. He emphasizes things like, "Safety is a priority," "We're going to be gospel-centered in our teaching," and "We're here to serve, not to dictate." God will get them to their destination, but the pastor is the driver steering and leading the passengers.

3. The pastor supports and encourages

The best leaders care well for those under their charge. Deliberate shepherding includes regular communication, problem solving, training, delegating, setting limits, and working as a liaison. The pastor's love is evident in how he comes alongside the staff and volunteers in the day-to-day work of caring for the church's children.

A pastor should set up regular meetings to talk through the state of the ministry. This provides rich opportunities for encouragement and to express thanks, a time to inquire about challenges and problem solve, a chance to talk through the bigger picture, and an occasion to train the staff.

The pastor can lend a hand in evaluating and managing the teachers. The majority of folks are great at following direction and teaching the curriculum. But things get dicey when a teacher does things her own way, ignores instructions from leaders, or worse, treats the children in the class poorly. Someone needs to have a hard conversation with this teacher. Our children's ministry leaders need to know they can call the pastor to help them walk through a difficult situation.

4. The pastor listens and communicates

The pastor ought to be accessible and available. If a volunteer suspects abuse, he needs to be able to quickly reach the pastor. If a staff member doesn't know what curriculum to choose, he or she can talk it over with the pastor. If the children's ministry director needs help to decide the maturity level of a member who recently volunteered, he or she could touch base with the pastor. The staff and church members can reach out whenever there is a need to talk, think things over, revise old plans, and make new ones.

5. The pastor solves problems

If there are not enough volunteers, if extra care is needed for a disabled child, if there is not an adequate evacuation plan, or if one child is bullying his peers, the pastor applies his wisdom, experience, and skill to these problems. The pastor and staff keep at it until the issue is resolved or progress is made.

The pastor leads his staff through these uncertainties and difficulties. He thinks and searches for solutions to current problems. His attentiveness and involvement demonstrate his love and care for the children's ministry team. They're not facing these problems alone. Their shepherd cares and wants to help.

When children's ministry leaders can turn to their pastor for help, they are less weighed down by their day-to-day challenges. For example, a pastor can help by recruiting volunteers from the pulpit. He can cast a vision for working with children—which is a great encouragement to a ministry in need of extra hands. Even though the children's ministry team is primarily responsible to recruit volunteers, the pastor's public support and willingness to help communicates his care. The pastor wants the children's ministry leaders to feel that he's willing to help anywhere he can.

6. The pastor trusts the team to do their work

There is no need to be a control freak or a micromanager. A pastor's goal is to equip the saints to do the work of the ministry, not do everything himself (Ephesians 4:11–16). He shows he's a wise pastor if he lets competent people do their job. He communicates his priorities and goals and then sets them free to execute.

7. The pastor sets healthy limits

Yes, that's right. A pastor needs to set limits on how much a worker can volunteer, to protect their spiritual well-being. Our priority is a believer's spiritual health, not a children's ministry program. If we overwork and burn out our staff and volunteers, what good is that for them (and us) in the long run? It might seem a convenient answer to task your children's ministry with providing childcare for a married couples meeting, but we must remember our folks are serving every Sunday and often midweek as well. Monitor how many services your volunteers are missing and think through how many meetings they should attend for their own spiritual growth.

The goal is to keep our servants protected from burnout. Who would you rather have in a classroom, a discouraged volunteer who's struggling because he's missed too much church serving week in and week out in children's ministry or a worker who is excited to bring all he is learning from the Sunday morning preaching into the children's ministry classroom? People will serve to their own detriment and that of the children if we let them. The pastor sets limits on how often a volunteer can serve so that they can regularly benefit and be fed by the Sunday morning preaching. Making a tough choice to limit the frequency of a teacher's service may require the children's ministry team to recruit additional help.

8. The pastor advocates

The pastor is a liaison for the staff and volunteers to the rest of the church's leadership team. He helps their concerns be heard and known. He speaks up when problems get big enough that they need direction from the entire board. He also works on behalf of the church's leadership to communicate their priorities to the children's ministry team.

9. The pastor engages hard things head-on

A good pastor will see a challenging situation, and rather than backing away out of fear or frustration, he takes charge of whatever is happening.

A pastor welcomes difficult conversations.

Natalia, a children's ministry director, was talking with Todd, a staff pastor. One of the little boys was getting physical with other children and disrespecting his Sunday school teachers. "He kicks, spits, and bites other kids and screams at the teachers," Natalia relayed with great concern.

"Give me the father's phone number, and I'll call him," Todd replied, without a moment's hesitation.

Does that surprise you? It doesn't surprise us. Why is that? It is the responsibility of pastors to take charge of difficult situations. This is an essential function of pastoral leadership, and it provides an opportunity to care for the flock. Todd didn't hesitate because he knows it's his responsibility to have the hard conversations with parents, especially the more ornery and prickly ones.

Let's shift situations. What if a sex offender showed up at the church? Or what if he called in advance to let someone know that he plans to attend the coming Sunday? The pastor should be the one to talk things over with the sex offender, informing him or her of the policy guidelines for sex offenders and sharing the limits of their participation. When a pastor is willing to take on these difficult conversations, it communicates his care to his children's ministry leaders.

A pastor makes unpopular decisions.

Our (Capitol Hill Baptist Church's) leadership is committed to letting our children's ministry be volunteer-driven. We've committed (as our church covenant says) to raise the children in the nurture and admonition of the Lord, by a pure and loving example. That statement is not just for the parents. That's everyone in the church—parents, singles, empty nesters, retired folks, and teenagers. As a church, we're *all* invested in children's ministry in one way or another.

One of the hard parts of living in Washington, DC, for me (Deepak) is that there is so much turnover in the city. Political professionals, military members, and youth (young urban professionals)—all add up to 10 to 20 percent of our church leaving every year. That means if we don't keep up with volunteer recruitment, we can quickly fall behind and not have enough volunteers to staff our needs.

If we don't have enough volunteers, I as the family ministry pastor bear the burden of enforcing unpopular but needed actions. We will shut down programs or enforce limits on the classrooms to ensure we have a good and safe environment for the children.

Picture this situation. Bob and Maxine Gladwell get their four children ready for church—feeding, changing diapers, and getting their children dressed. They shuffle the children into the van, drive twenty-five minutes to church, get them out of the van, and head over to the children's section of church. After a hectic and frustrating morning (which is common on Sundays!), the Gladwells find out that the three-year-old and six-year-olds' classrooms are closed because there are not enough volunteers. So, in a moment of frustration, Maxine raises her voice at the volunteer coordinator behind the desk and storms off with her kids in tow.

When the pastor (Todd) hears about this from the children's ministry director (Natalia) after the morning service, he picks up the phone and calls the Gladwells. While it's disappointing that there are not enough volunteers, the pastor can commiserate with these parents because his own kids didn't get into the same classes! And yet, as he tells the parents, there is no excuse to raise one's voice at the volunteers. As pastors, we shouldn't pass off these difficult conversations to our volunteers. We must be willing to enforce hard and unpopular decisions and to take responsibility for them.

The Reward

When a pastor cares for the children's ministry leaders by limiting their workload and leading through difficult situations, he makes their service a joy. When they know they can rely on the pastor to help them think through challenges and raise issues at a regular meeting, they won't feel overwhelmed. The end result is that the key workers will stick around. I (Marty) am still serving at the same church and still leading children's ministry; it's been thirty-three years now. In that time, I've only had four couples coordinating our ministry to children under me.

Trust me, it is a whole lot easier to care for your leaders and keep them spiritually healthy by doing the things described above than to try and recruit and start over with a new leader every other year. If you haven't been giving your children's ministry leaders the proper care and you are wondering where to begin, start by inviting them out for over a meal to encourage them and draw them out for ways you can help. Chances are they will stick around.

Self-Evaluation: Pastors Lead and Shepherd

Pastors: Is there anything in this chapter that you are *not* doing? If so, how would you feel about adding that into your leadership of the children's ministry?

Children's ministry staff or volunteers: The temptation is to read this chapter and think, *Gosh, that's not what my pastor does. I don't get support like this!* If you feel like your pastor is falling short, avoid the temptation to feel bitter or frustrated. The place to start is to pray that the Lord would give direction and wisdom to the leaders of your church. Nothing changes unless we first take time to pray.

5. Children's Ministry Directors Organize and Execute

Adrianna stood up and was about to walk out of the Sunday school class, but I (Deepak) asked her, "Do you have a moment to talk?" She nodded in agreement and paused.

I started with, "Have you ever had a conversation that might change the direction of your life?"

Her eyebrows raised and she looked startled. I'm sure she thought, *Gosh, what does he mean?*

Over the next few minutes, I explained to Adrianna that pastors were wondering if she would consider the role of children's ministry director. She worked in a secular job for the last two decades and never worked for a church before. Understandably, she was surprised by my inquiry. The natural question tumbled out of her mouth: "Why me?"

I explained to Adrianna the qualities we saw in her that would make for a good staff member and an excellent children's ministry director. The person serving as your children's ministry director (CMD) is the muscle and brawn behind the scenes that make things happen day in and day out in children's ministry. That allows the pastor overseeing children's ministry to concentrate on shepherding the members involved and remain involved in big-picture leadership. We (the pastors) saw in Adrianna a faithful, humble, hard-working member who would make a great addition to our team.

In this chapter, we'll explain the ideal qualities and job description of a CMD and how to care for them. (Remember, this list outlines the ideal. We rarely get our ideal in this fallen world. That is what discipleship is all about. It allows you to deploy someone in need of coaching and training.) We'll also tackle ways to help prevent burnout and high turnover of your CMD.

An Ideal Children's Ministry Director

Let's say your church is looking to hire a children's ministry director. Ramona shows up. She's thoughtful and friendly. She loves Jesus and is a hard worker. She's interested in this job. What makes for a good children's ministry director?

Two essential qualities

Further down we'll cover several skill sets and responsibilities related to this role, but let's start with two necessary qualities. If your candidate doesn't have these two, then don't bother working through the job description with them. It's a waste of your time! (Note: This example involves a woman, but we've seen this role filled by a man or woman or even a couple!)

A children's ministry director must be a *born-again Christian* (John 3:3). Ramona should be a godly woman who feverishly and fervently loves Christ. If you're sticking her in front of your children weekly to model the gospel and Christian faith, you want to make sure she's got a vibrant faith, not a fledgling one.

A children's ministry director should be *a member of your church*. She's more than a hired gun; she's God's child who desperately needs God's grace. Ramona is a fellow church member who has covenanted to fight for faith and care for these children. You want your ministry's top leaders to be shaped and molded by the preaching in your church. Regular participation in the worship service positions your children's ministry director to pass on the senior pastor's vision to your children.

Should your children's ministry director be single or married?

It is not a requirement that your children's ministry director be married or have children. You might think, *It would be great to have a mom or dad (or both) because they'll have personal experience in raising children.* A mom or dad may have a more mature view of kids, but they may also be overrun with commitments to their family (1 Corinthians 7:34). A single person (without children) has greater flexibility of schedule and can perhaps remain more focused on the task, and is far less likely to get pulled away. However, she might overwork herself. She might use her freedom and flexibility to overextend herself.

Expectations for a children's ministry director

What should comprise a CMD's typical job description? Consider these seven responsibilities. Note: Don't panic if you realize your children's ministry director has a few weaknesses or limitations as you read this list. Delegate some of the following tasks to a second person. For example, you could have a curriculum coordinator who serves the children's ministry director. Though, keep in mind, the first expectation on this list is critical.

1. Administrative

There is a reason this one is first. Your CMD is responsible for keeping the ministry running. Administration is the engine that keeps the machine running smoothly. So, your CMD should be able to troubleshoot problems with grace. She should be organized but also flexible and good with logistics. She's so good, she could coordinate the fifth battalion of the US Marines or coordinate your children's ministry, and she's graciously chosen the latter.

2. Takes initiative

In choosing a CMD, look for a person who gets things done. A CMD takes action, organizes, plans, and executes without needing you to direct them each step of the way. When I (Marty) began serving as our children's pastor, the nuts and bolts of running our children's ministry took a ton of time. I spent time buying pretzels, recruiting substitutes, and calling people when we had a case of lice in one of our classrooms. Today, our entire operation functions without me. Unless there is an out-of-the-ordinary challenge, the children's ministry staff doesn't call me. That allows me to focus my attention on our ministry's big-picture vision, writing curriculum, and providing pastoral care for our workers and families.

3. Curriculum coordinator

Ramona (on behalf of the church) purchases curriculum for the Sunday school teachers or children's church workers. She knows what to look for in a curriculum—that a good curriculum is gospel-rich, biblically minded, and lines up with the chief priorities of your church.

4. Teacher-trainer

Ramona doesn't just buy the curriculum but also ensures that it's taught in a developmentally thoughtful and engaging way. The worst thing a CMD can do is dump a curriculum on the teachers and say, "Good luck." Oftentimes, volunteers are not professional teachers nor summer camp directors, but mailmen, lawyers, accountants, plumbers, and taxi drivers (in my—Deepak's—case, one of the children's ministry hall monitors was also the director of the Secret Service! Needless to say, we felt secure when he was around). So, the CMD trains the volunteers to (for example) manage a classroom of two dozen toddlers. Training is an important tool in the CMD's arsenal!

5. Event planner

Every Sunday service is a big event for your ministry. There is a lot of energy, effort, and thought that goes into a Sunday. Children's ministry pulls together loads of volunteers, teaching, activities, games, food, and much more!

If you expect your CMD to run a Vacation Bible School, remember that a VBS is children's ministry on steroids for an entire, action-packed, breathtaking, nonstop week. You'll need a person who is a gifted event planner to pull together a VBS.

6. Recruiter

As volunteers either move away or jump to another church ministry, your CMD works to find replacements. An effective CMD has a heart to recruit, support, and encourage. Volunteers are not just warm bodies. They are image bearers who have worries, heartaches, and troubles. The CMD cares for them; she's doesn't use them. Though the CMD takes responsibility for general recruiting, every ministry runs into seasons when you experience a more significant deficit of workers.

At my (Marty's) church, we lost thirty children's ministry leaders and workers when we sent out a large church plant. They were some of our best people. Due to the great need, our whole leadership team got involved in a push to fill the gaps left in sending some of our best to the church plant.

7. Policy-enforcer

Like a law enforcement officer, the CMD maintains the "law of the land" and reinforces the ministry policies and procedures. Policies are needed—everything from universal health and safety precautions to bathroom guidelines. Your CMD is the primary person concerned about whether the church teachers and volunteers are abiding by the policies. Volunteers won't always remember what they're supposed to do, so they'll ask the CMD.

Timmy, a twentysomething single man teaching in a first grade Sunday school class, asks Ramona, "What's the bathroom policy again?" or "What do you do when a child doesn't do what you ask?" What an opportunity! Ramona gets to teach this volunteer how to correct a child in a loving, appropriate way. What an excellent opportunity for that young man to learn from a seasoned children's ministry leader.

Consider these seven parts of the CMD's job description. To get all this done, Ramona either needs to be Superwoman, or she needs to depend daily on God's grace and the charity of the church. There's a lot here, and if we're not careful, we'll run her into the ground. How do we set reasonable expectations, help Ramona to get her job done, and not run her ragged?

How to Prevent Burnout of Your Children's Ministry Director

With tears in her eyes, Janelle shared on our phone call, "I can't do it anymore."

Mid-thirties, married with two kiddos of her own, Janelle has been working as the children's ministry director of a mid-size church in the Midwest. She was supposed to be part-time, but it was closer to full-time work many weeks because there was so much to do. On most days, she loves her job, but the last year has been rough.

Like a battle-fatigued soldier, Janelle didn't have anything left to give. Here's what added up to her downfall:

- She is consistently short of volunteers. She's desperate for help and doesn't feel the congregation is supportive. They don't understand how much need there is in the children's ministry.
- If something goes wrong on a Sunday, like a volunteer getting sick at the last minute, she's stays as a backup. She's constantly plugging holes in an ever-leaking dam.
- She doesn't have anyone helping her oversee the children's ministry on Sundays. It is pretty much *The Janelle Show*. She calls the shots, organizes the volunteers, sets up things in advance, and wipes down and cleans things afterward.
- All this adds up to her rarely making it to church services to hear the sermon. She can't remember the last time she was able to sit through the entire church service uninterrupted.
- The pastoral leadership rarely pays attention to children's ministry or her work and doesn't realize she is struggling. No one is complaining, and everyone loves Janelle.

- She seldom takes a vacation or gets a break. She's present and working fifty or fifty-one out of fifty-two weeks a year.
- Her church involvement is reduced to just children's ministry. She's good at what she does, but that's *all* she does in her church. She's not a part of a small group. She didn't join a Bible study when offered. She hardly ever meets up with other Christian women for fellowship or accountability.

Janelle is overworked and underappreciated—no wonder she is ready to throw in the towel.

For the past few months, there was a tick, tick, tick, tick, tick sounding in your children's ministry, and you missed picking up on it. She's been a walking time bomb, ready to implode at any future moment. Unless you step in quickly with some help, Janelle will become another in a long list of CMD casualties.

How you ever noticed the high turnover in the CMD position in your church? Why doesn't the CMD stick around for ten or twenty years? If you're the CMD, can you relate to Janelle's story? What kind of love, training, and support would make the Janelles of this world stick around longer?

We'll offer six suggestions for how to care for Janelle and ensure she never becomes overwhelmed. This list is not meant to be comprehensive. Whether you're a pastor, the CMD, or a parent, you'll need to think creatively about how to make adjustments and tailor it for your context. But these suggestions will help provoke your thinking about how to keep your CMD emotionally and spiritually healthy over the long-term.

1. Shepherd the CMD's soul, not just their job

As a pastor or leader responsible for children's ministry, the single most important task you have is the care of the servants who carry out the work. Keep them healthy and happy, and it will go well for your ministry.

Though Janelle needs to get her job done, the most vital thing about her life is not her job—it's her soul. She is foremost a born-again Christian, a child of God, and a new creation in Christ. A CMD will often choose to fill in gaps, work overtime, and take on responsibilities neglected by others to her own detriment. Sometimes, there will be crazy Sundays when it seems like nothing went according to plan, and your CMD had to jump in to bail water. But if she is bailing every Sunday, someone needs to be aware. If you are her pastor, that someone is you.

Keep in mind that your CMD has struggles outside the classroom too. She might be doing a top-notch job as a director—parents are happy, volunteers are doing good work, and the children love attending the church's kids' programs. But if the CMD's job performance is an A+, but her soul is a D-, then we're failing her. We can and must do better. We should care more about her relationship with Christ than her job performance. Who she is in Christ matters far more than what she does for him. Jesus cares about whether Janelle loves him. We should care enough to ask Janelle regularly, "How is your relationship with Christ?" or "How are you growing in your love for Jesus?" Asking such things shows that her spiritual life really does matter.

Make sure Janelle is growing in the Word and seeking out her Savior. Encourage and point to her hope in Christ. Plead with her to trust that Christ is sufficient for her troubles. Fortify her with truth when the Evil One discourages her or tempts her to doubts. Pray for her and with her.

How ironic it would be for Janelle to grow bitter against Jesus (and her church) while she's working full-time as the CMD in her church. This, then, is our first goal: to make sure our CMD maintains a vibrant love for her Savior.

2. The CMD must be generous in giving responsibility to the members

Janelle can't do everything. If she attempts to do everything, she will crumble under the weight of responsibility. So why is it that a CMD would try? Maybe it's because a misplaced sense of faithfulness, or her identity is wrapped up in the position. Or it could be she is not effective at delegating. Other times, a CMD is withering under the leaders' or parents' high expectations for children's ministry. Regardless of the reason, when a CMD does everything, it's not healthy. We need to help our CMD hand over as much responsibility as is possible to the members of the church.

The last thing you want is the CMD to be a control freak and the solution to every problem. Help Janelle set a goal to give away enough responsibility to other gifted helpers such that her role shifts to more of an NFL commissioner. She's coordinating and overseeing different "coaches" and "teams" rather than being the sole person running the entire show. She's not shy, but she's aggressive in giving out opportunities to others.

When Adrianna (my church's CMD) came to me (Deepak) and asked if she could visit her sister on a weekend and miss a Sunday service, I shouted, "Oh my goodness, Yes!" Adrianna was surprised by my exuberance. I thought, *What a golden opportunity.* I wanted Adrianna to see that our children's ministry program would be healthier if it could run without her present. That would be a good sign that we weren't overly dependent on her for our programs to work. The CMD should give away responsibilities such that children's ministry should be able to run without the CMD around, which leads us to our next suggestion.

3. Build a competent and talented team around your CMD

The FBI and CIA have their little secrets. We're going to give you one of ours. Ready? Are you sitting down? *Deacons can transform your children's ministry.*[1] In the Bible, the term "deacon" refers to an officer of the church (like a pastor/elder) and describes one who serves a specific need on behalf of the church. In Acts 6, when the needs of widows were being neglected, the apostles gathered together the disciples and picked seven "full of the Spirit and wisdom" (v. 3) to take care of this practical need.

Volunteers are a wonderful help but are not always stable over the course of years. When assembling a volunteer ministry, people can come and go as they please because there is no formal office to which they are assigned.

However, a more formal leadership team can stabilize your children's ministry over the long haul. For some churches, this means developing deacon roles alongside the CMD. For other churches, it might be hiring one or two part-time paid positions. Others may create unique roles for their situation, like a nursery coordinator or teacher trainer for your Sunday school teachers. Build a team of competent people around the CMD who take ownership of the ministry.

You might think in terms of a sheriff who deputizes one or two people in his community to assist in fighting crime—he formally gives them the responsibility to work alongside him. He sticks a star on their shirt and takes them along on the next crime investigation.

This is our third goal: Have your "sheriff" CMD deputize enough members to build a team of people to help run children's ministry. Don't ever let your CMD stand alone as the sole leader.

Here are two practical tips on building a children's ministry team. First, look for a gifted assistant to your CMD, someone who can train to take over the ministry when your CMD is away or is ill. Today is the best day to begin the preparation for tomorrow's transition. Your ministry can run like a football team. If the quarterback goes down, the coach doesn't take over. He sends in the backup. The backup studies the playbook and helps monitor the defense from the sidelines in every game. He is ready to take over within minutes. Who is the backup quarterback for your CMD?

Secondly, your backup needs a backup. At my church (Marty), we have a CMD, an assistant to the CMD, and a team of coordinators over various age groups. If the CMD goes down, the backup steps in, and one of the coordinators step into the backup role. Should our CMD have a family emergency, for example, the entire process happens without pastoral involvement. That frees me as the family ministries pastor to care for the CMD while the ministry continues without interruption.

4. Make sure your children's ministry leadership team is made up of active and healthy members of your church

Don't let the spiritual life of Janelle, her backups, and any key leaders revolve exclusively around their jobs in children's ministry. That's a quick way to suffocate them spiritually. There is more to Janelle and her team than children's ministry.

Why ensure that the folks on your team are all members of your church? The membership process ensures that you get to know folks before placing them in leadership positions.[2] Membership makes them accountable to your church leadership. It is also a great way to ensure a predator cannot quickly fill a position as a leader in your ministry. If you hire a person outside the security of knowing them through a long-standing membership history, he or she has skirted around a robust character screening. If they are relatively new to your congregation, it will be helpful to find out if they were an active, healthy member of their last church.

As a church member, Janelle made a conscious commitment to this local body of believers, to come alongside other members. She helps them grow in Christ, and they likewise help her. They coexist as a spiritual cooperative, encouraging one another to persevere and journey toward heaven together.

If Janelle spends all of her time on the children's ministry floors but never makes it into the main worship services, she'll never hear the sermon. She'll wither away spiritually if she's not fed consistently. Hearing the sermon is like eating a nutritious meal—it keeps her spiritually healthy. If she doesn't eat a healthy meal each Sunday, she'll starve. If she never gets to sing with the congregation, pray along with the corporate prayers, or hear the pastor's sermon, she doesn't realign her heart with spiritual truth. God has established a weekly rhythm for Janelle's life—attending a Sunday worship service resets Janelle and prepares her to face the trials and tribulations of the coming week. *Make sure your CMD can regularly participate in the church's worship services.*

Janelle sees the church volunteers, parents, and children regularly because of her job. She has pleasant but superficial interactions. Rarely does anyone asks her, "How are you doing spiritually?" Like every believer, she needs a close friendship with others who know her life and keep her accountable. She should have a few people who know her joys and burdens, hopes and dreams, frustrations and desires. She sharpens other women spiritually, and they sharpen her. Her closest Christian friends challenge her to confess her sin, dig deep into the Word, and trust her Savior when things get hard. But she can't do that if her life revolves around her job and all of her relationships at church are superficial. *Make sure your CMD is growing in her relationship with other believers in the church.*

We've emphasized the public gatherings and her personal connections, but be sure Janelle is evangelizing, showing hospitality, and doing anything that normal members should do.

5. Lavish an abundance of encouragement on the CMD

Are you stingy with your support for your CMD? What would it be like for Janelle to feel fully and completely supported and loved by her pastoral leadership? When you meet with your CMD, do you take time to thank them for their work? If we had a balance scale and put your encouragements like weights on one side of the scale, would they far outweigh your adjustments and corrections? That is the goal.

Here are additional ways you can encourage your CMD.

Trust Janelle's judgment. If you're the pastor, and you've entrusted her with a job to do, then don't undermine her. If you tell her, "Do job A, and I don't have any preferences," then you should not manipulate, rearrange, or redo her work. If you do that, you show that you really don't trust her.

When things are hard, be there for her. Don't leave her to fight battles on her own. Make sure she knows that you will support her, especially when things get tough.

Protect Janelle from "darts and arrows" she'll face in her role. When parents get mad or other staff get frustrated, don't let them vent on or berate Janelle. Step in the way when it's appropriate—have the hard conversations for her whenever you can. An excellent way to stay abreast of these challenging moments is to require that your CMD report conflict or problems the same day. That allows the pastor to step in. If a parent blows up at your CMD, it creates a pastoral opportunity to care. Often it reveals a deeper issue in one or both of their lives that requires shepherding, not administration.

Give constant encouragement. Be especially clear when Janelle does things well—give her affirmation for a job well done. And find big and small ways to offer encouragement. My (Deepak's) three daughters discovered that our CMD (Adrianna) loves apple cinnamon-flavored fig bars. The next time we were at the grocery store, Noelle and Eden said, "Daddy, look!" They were pointing to a pack of—yes, you guessed it—apple cinnamon fig bars. We bought a box of them, and once every other week, the girls stop by and give Adrianna a little two-pack of fig bars. It's not earth-shattering. It doesn't radically change her world. But it's a small gesture of kindness, a simple way to say to her, "We love and appreciate you."

Look to host events to encourage the entire team and thank them for their service. Every year, I (Marty) invite our children's ministry team to our home for a summer picnic. We host a Christmas dinner each December. During these times, we enjoy a meal, play a few games, and I take the opportunity to thank them for their service with gifts. I do an overnight retreat at a local bed and breakfast for our core leadership team in the spring. During that short retreat, we share meals, review a chapter or two from a book that I've given them ahead of time, and then spend an hour or so reviewing the state of the ministry and brainstorming new ideas that will allow us to improve and grow. These times help build the team's health, make them feel encouraged and appreciated, and help tremendously with leader retention. Whenever someone considers stepping down from their position, I want it to be a struggle, knowing that they are going to greatly miss the regular encouragement and blessings that come with leading in children's ministry.

6. Make sure your CMD takes a break

Having all work and no breaks is not healthy for anyone's soul, let alone a CMD. Do everything you can to make sure they take a break from the everyday pressures of their job.

Sundays are often hectic, with children's programs running throughout the day. A CMD works much of Sunday—there is a need to be present in the children's ministry and get things done on Sundays.

Thus, give your CMD, if she's a full-time employee, a lot of flexibility on Monday, ideally by taking that day off. Let Janelle slow down and get some rest, especially since Sundays are not restful. Let her catch up on personal Bible study, responsibilities at home, or time with friends.

If your CMD is a volunteer or receives a small stipend, you can't treat her as a full-time employee. If you compensate Janelle for serving on Sundays, don't assume she can also cover childcare for a married couples meeting or that she will be in charge of your summer VBS. It is challenging to shoulder children's ministry on top of another full-time job. In my (Marty's) church, our (volunteer) CMD only leads our Sunday ministry. We've got another leader over our midweek programs and a third person who runs our VBS. With 250+ children in our Sunday morning program, our CMD doesn't have the capacity to take on the midweek childcare. He and his wife have a family of their own and volunteer to lead our children's ministry. We give them a small monthly stipend as a thank you. Because we have not overloaded them, they've been serving as CMDs for a decade.

Make sure your CMD takes vacation time. Let's say Janelle is working year-round, with little to no breaks. Get her to periodically step away from the daily pressures. No email. No phone calls. Lots of extra sleep. A fun and edifying fiction book. Lots of laughs. A few board games or a replay of her favorite movie. Tell her to go out to dinner with her family or for long walks with her husband. This is the stuff that makes for a good break from the stress of normal life.

A Healthy CMD Makes for a Better Children's Ministry

While we don't have an answer for solving every church's problems, the recipe for a healthy CMD is not that hard to figure out. Keep Janelle grounded in Christ. Be sure to feed her spiritually. Don't ever leave her isolated and alone in her responsibilities. Help build a solid team of people around her. Encourage delegation to the members of your church. Encourage, encourage, and then encourage some more in whatever she sets her hand to.

To God be the glory. As we care well for our CMD, we serve the whole church, not just Janelle.

Self-Evaluation: CMD Burnout

Pastors: Does your CMD seem burned out? If so, what adjustments do you need to make?

CMD: Do you read the job description and think, *I'm doing too much*, or *I don't think I can handle everything*? Are you emotionally and spiritually exhausted? Where do you need to pass off responsibility to members? Can you build a competent team around you, and if so, what steps do you need to take? Are you getting into the church services regularly to hear the sermon and pray with the congregation?

Parents: Can you go to your CMD and ask, "What can I do to help?" (Be careful, he or she might fall out of their chair, since no one ever asks that question!)

6. Members Maintain Children's Ministry

Sally is sixty-eight years old and African American. She's about the kindest woman you'd ever meet on the planet. She's been teaching the kindergarten Sunday school class in the same church for thirty years. She's had four different pastors, and she'll probably outlast the next two or three.

James is twenty-one and Korean. He's a senior at the University of Wisconsin. He volunteers in childcare in the two-year-olds' classroom. He likes reading stories to the kids and working on puzzles with them. You'll often find several kids around him while he reads through *The Big Picture Story Bible*.

José is thirty-five and Latino. He's a foreman at Sherman's construction company during the week. On Sundays, he's a hall monitor on the children's ministry hallway once or twice a month. His first job is to make sure the floors stay safe, but he's also an extra set of hands if a teacher needs help.

Sarah is forty-five and Caucasian. She's got teenagers. She likes serving alongside her daughters Lydia and Eden in the baby and infants' room. She misses having babies in her house!

Sally, James, José, and Sarah are at the same local church, Cornerstone Bible Church in Suneville, Wisconsin. As a church, they've committed to being invested in one another. There's a strong sense of community at Cornerstone Bible—people really care about what's going on with their fellow members. Pastor James Johnson often says from the pulpit, "Don't live this Christian life alone! Be sure you're doing life with the believers around you."

Once a month in their worship service, the members of Cornerstone stand and recite the words of their church covenant. A covenant is a short summary of how the members intend to live as Christians. Halfway through the covenant, it states, "We will endeavor to lead those in our care in the nurture and admonition of the Lord, as well as to seek the salvation of our family and friends." This line doesn't just apply to parents but every member of the church. As Sally would often tell the young women she disciples, "As a church, we take responsibility for each other, and that includes the little ones."

The apostle Paul compared the church to a body with each part serving in keeping with the gifts the Lord bestowed:

> For as in one body we have many members, and the members do not all have the same function, so we, though many, are one body in Christ, and individually members one of another. Having gifts that differ according to the grace given to us, let us use them: if prophecy, in proportion to our faith; if service, in our serving; the one who teaches, in his teaching; the one who exhorts, in his exhortation; the one who contributes, in generosity; the one who leads, with zeal; the one who does acts of mercy, with cheerfulness. (Romans 12:4–8)

Different folks have different gifts, but it takes everyone working together to enable the body to function well. When you consider that the average children's ministry is composed of 20 to 25 percent of the neediest attenders of your church (the kids), it is easy to see how it is an "all hands on deck" operation! For you to have a thriving children's ministry, your members must be willing to do their part. Parents have an incentive to build a gospel-centered children's ministry because they want their kids to know the truth. But they can't be the only members to contribute! *For the children's ministry to thrive, we need other members (not just the parents) to jump in.*

Pastors cast a vision for the next generation that can mobilize members to serve. The children's ministry staff are the hands and feet on the ground, organizing and executing to make children's ministry happen. And if the staff builds the trellis, the members show up and do the work of teaching, instructing, and watching over the children. It's the normal, everyday members that keep the children's ministry going by their presence, energy, and loving efforts. They're the gas in the engine that makes the whole thing run.

Perhaps your church is functioning well like the work at Cornerstone, or maybe you've just taken over the ministry and need to do a complete overhaul. You've got a half-dozen committed teachers, but that's it. Every Sunday, you try to pull in enough extra hands to meet the minimum requirements for two adults in the classroom. You need more volunteers, but you're not sure where to begin.

What does it take to recruit, train, nurture, and retain volunteers so that we can build a vibrant children's ministry? That's the topic we'll cover in this chapter. Talk to any coach of a division 1 college sports team and you'll hear him or her say, "A program lives or dies by who it recruits." The same goes for children's ministry. If you don't recruit well for children's ministry, you'll eventually run into trouble.

Various Approaches to Recruiting

There are a variety of ways to recruit volunteers. As you'll see, some of them are problematic, based on panic or a sense of guilt, while others are more holistic and helpful, focusing on nurturing a vision for ministry to the next generation. Let's see how Ramona (the children's ministry director at Cornerstone Bible Church) might recruit members.

The twisting arms approach

Ramona can beg, berate, or guilt members into participating. However, in our experience, this won't prove fruitful in the long run. If she forces members to be involved, she'll have high attrition rates, which means her recruiting problem never goes away. Those arm-twisted members will show up late or not show up at all. They didn't want to be there in the first place, and they don't know why they have to serve.

Sounding the alarm

Sounding the alarm sounds something like this: "We're DESPERATE for more help in the elementary school classes. Unless we get help, we're going to need to shut things down. We CAN'T KEEP GOING if we don't get more help!" (Picture Ramona with tears in her eyes and perspiration running down her forehead.)

If she sounds panicked every time she asks for help, her church eventually grows tone-deaf to her pleas. Recurring desperate threats of closing the ministry come across as her crying wolf. No one believes she would shut things down. Her alarm becomes like the train whistle that blows from nearby tracks; soon, you don't even hear it.

The pay-for-play method

She can pay for church members to watch the kids. Compensation for childcare is not morally wrong; in fact, it's appropriate if you are babysitting your neighbor's kids while they go out on a date. However, if the church's leaders set up a system of compensation in exchange for volunteer time, this diminishes the sense of responsibility members have for each other, including kids in their church community. The members who show up need extra income; they're not exclusively motivated by gospel sacrifices. Compensation usurps members' gospel motivations.

While all these methods can put warm bodies in the classroom, none solve your bigger problem—to give your children the best gospel-motivated care and instruction your church can provide. So, what's left?

Inform, inspire, and pray

Children's ministry is like any other gospel ministry. If Ramona wants folks to be excited to participate, she has got to inform them of the need and inspire them to join in the opportunity. That is how we lead people to give toward a building fund, evangelize, invite their neighbors to church, and how we motivate them to come in early to help set out chairs on Sunday morning as part of the setup crew.

Before your members sign up to serve with children, they will need information. How many children are in the church? What is the vision of the ministry—the end goal that informs the type of care and instruction you want to provide? What is the need—how many open slots do you have? The aim is to invite them into the process and welcome their prayers. Ramona wants the congregation to know that staffing children's ministry is not "someone else's problem." Rather, she wants them to see it as "our opportunity and calling."

The best way to inform the church is to give periodic updates on the ministry. Share updates on Sunday mornings, through quarterly email updates, in your Sunday printed bulletin, or at your members' meeting. Remember to add encouragement and variety to keep people listening. You don't want the church to just hear about your need for more volunteers; otherwise they'll tune Ramona out. They should hear the testimonies of what God is doing and how the Lord has provided. You'll get those remaining slots filled faster when you inspire your congregation.

Ramona (alongside her pastor James Johnson) can inspire her church with this gospel opportunity. Many of the children are not Christians. They come along with their parents, listening, and participating in the children's programs. Over the course of many years, this will be the most consistent evangelistic opportunity offered to the church.

Ramona should also tell your members that this is a growth opportunity. Any time God asks us to serve others, it's a chance to deny our selfishness and, in humility, learn to put others first (Philippians 2:3–4). We want to see ministry the way God does—as service to the entire body. When each part of the body does its part, the body grows, as it builds itself up in love (Ephesians 4:16). God shapes and molds these church members into his image by what he asks them to do, including serving in children's ministry.[1]

There is no need to panic, manipulate, or beg for help. If Ramona's confidence is in God and she's not fearful, then all that's needed is an even-keeled request for help. She makes the needs clear to the church. Remind the members of their commitment to raise these kids together. Pray for God's provision. And then trust him to bring adequate workers to meet the needs.

Once Cornerstone Bible Church is informed and inspired, they will respond to the need. From there, Ramona will still need to recruit to fill the remaining positions. But it is far easier to ask particular individuals to fill a specific role because she believes they are a good fit than it is asking anyone to please do anything.

Self-Evaluation: What's your approach to recruiting?

Slow down and consider for a moment—which approach do you most often employ when seeking to mobilize volunteers? Do you trust God with the recruiting, or do you walk around fretting constantly about it? How might you adjust your heart disposition so that you can offer a more even-keeled approach?

Additional Tips for Recruitment

The pastors at Cornerstone try to catch members on the front end of joining the church before they get too busy with other ministries (e.g., hospitality, greeting, sound ministry, security). A pastor will ask a prospective member if he or she is willing to serve in childcare during their membership interview. They gauge interest early.

If church leaders get behind recruitment, it makes a difference. When the senior pastor James speaks, he carries a weight and authority accrued to him from being the lead shepherd. There is power and influence in the pulpit. Thus, when pastor James says, "Come and help with the kids," people will listen.

If Ramona works at a highly transient church, recruiting will be crucial to her survival. For example, as we mentioned in chapter 4, Capitol Hill Baptist Church (CHBC) sits in the middle of urban Washington, DC, and turns over 10 to 20 percent of the members every year. We have a new church every five years or so. The Sallys of the world, who teach the same Sunday school class for decades, just don't exist in our congregation. If the children's ministry director doesn't constantly recruit, the needs will outpace the volunteer capacity, and CHBC quickly falls behind and runs the risk of having to shut down children's programs.

Jonathan is pastor of a small church in Wannona, South Dakota, and as he tells it, "People rarely leave our town. They usually live in our community for their entire lives, so we rarely see people leave our church community." Their turnover is about 2 to 5 percent every year. If you are in a church with little to no turnover, recruiting will be important to get "fresh blood" in front of the kids. You want new faces, which brings along new energy and new ideas.

An every-parent-serves model

What happens when Ramona does everything that's described—inform, inspire, ask, and pray—and her church is still falling short of volunteers? Though our preferred way to recruit is for members to volunteer of their own volition, there are times when Ramona might need to require members to serve.

At one point my (Marty's) church grew so quickly that our needs in children's ministry quickly outpaced our capacity. Children twelve and under made up a third of our church attendance. We realized that even if every parent served, it would only cover 80 percent of the teaching and helping slots. That was when we asked every parent with kids in the ministry to serve in rotation. We deployed those gifted and willing to teach as teachers. The remaining parents took on helper roles where no prep was needed. That gave us the adequate coverage we needed to ensure our classrooms were safe. It took the senior pastor and other leaders to lead the charge and explain the need to successfully transition from an all-volunteer model to an every-parent-serves model.

The amazing byproduct of our efforts was getting more dads involved. Before that move, most of our classes were staffed by moms and grandmoms, with only a sprinkling of dads. After we got every parent involved, dads made up about a third of our teachers. Children's ministry suddenly turned into a discipleship opportunity for our fathers. As they watched our most seasoned teacher teach our kids the Bible on Sunday, they learned how to teach their own children the rest of the week. Though children's ministry needs are not currently as overwhelming, we've kept the every-parent-serves model, and our children's ministry continues to serve as a training ground for our new dads.

A deacon of recruitment

Several years ago, I (Deepak) created a volunteer position in the children's ministry exclusively dedicated to recruitment. This resourceful member comes alongside the children's ministry staff and facilitates recruiting of volunteers. Whenever a church member says, "Yes, I'll serve," this deacon of recruitment facilitates members getting integrated into children's ministry. A member can't just walk in the door and start serving. Because child abuse is common, we do background checks and screening applications before a person serves. Before prospective volunteers get in front of the kids, we also require an initial training session. Each of these steps (background check, application, initial training) can create a bottleneck in our recruiting of volunteers. Somebody's got to gently nudge the members along, helping them not get stuck in the bottleneck. That's our deacon of recruitment. As our current deacon, Trevor, made abundantly clear, "Assigning one person to recruiting means someone will feel the pressure of getting results and will make a sincere effort and face hard questions on why recruits aren't coming in."

Train and Retrain Your Volunteers

Ramona can't throw volunteers into a room and expect that most will naturally know what to do. Sure, some are parents, but that doesn't mean that the volunteers (even the parents) know how to handle everything. She trains to impart vision, principles, and practicalities for children's ministry.

Ramona equips volunteers to be faithful stewards of the gospel opportunities with the children. She never recruits and leaves them to figure it out on their own. If she asks them to serve, she walks alongside them throughout their service, giving them what they need.[2]

What we train

What does Ramona tell the volunteers when she trains them?

She reminds them about safety and protection measures. Do they know what to do if a boy is repeatedly biting other children? Can they evacuate the children out of the building in the case of a fire? The first goal is to keep the kids secure, whether it's an internal problem (like a kid hitting another kid) or external (like a man who shows up with a gun).

She sets out the goals of what they're striving for, like keeping kids safe and raising up the next generation of godly young men and women for God's glory. As deacon Trevor put it, "If you tell people they're babysitting for two and a half hours a month, that's going to yield people running out the clock in their roles. If you tell them they're protecting and advancing our gospel witness and showing God glory through their service, you're more likely to win new recruits and see them serve vigilantly."

Ramona offers a full picture of what's involved. She does as best she can to give volunteers a clear sense of what she's asking them to do so there are no major surprises.

She instructs in behavior management. If kids are jumping on tables, running around like crazy people, and throwing chalk, the volunteer doesn't know how to manage a crowd. Teach them basic classroom techniques in overseeing a group of children.

She sharpens their communication skills. Can they teach a Bible story in a way that's thoughtful, content-driven, yet also engaging for the children?

She teaches about how to *prevent and respond to abuse.* Evil people want to hurt the children. We demonstrate wisdom when we strategize how to prevent abuse and respond to it wisely when and if it does show up in our church. Do the volunteers know whom to talk to if they witness or suspect abuse? Are there policies and procedures that guide the staff, or is there an ad hoc response?

Ramona teaches how to respond to emergencies—how to evacuate during a fire, what to do if a tornado strikes, how to react if an active shooter walks in, and so on.

She offers training, but the reality is—people will eventually forget much of what we tell them. It might be frustrating, but it's true. That's why she retrains again, again, and again.

How we train

Much of the children's ministries' training can be done on the job. When Ramona adds a new person to a team, she assigns them to a helper role with little responsibility other than watching over the children in a classroom under a seasoned helper. Ramona instructs an experienced worker to train the new volunteer over the course of the year. Once she gets this mentoring system up and running, it can largely perpetuate itself. An experienced worker can pass on the day's schedule, tips for classroom management, the best way to read and act out a Bible story, and the proper bathroom procedures to follow. Over the course of a year, a new helper will be in a position to take on their own apprentice.

Teachers learn from each other. They benefit immensely from this mentor system, which pairs rookies with experienced teachers. Before the class, the teachers do a pre-session, highlighting what will happen, any children that require extra attention, and teaching tips. During class, the rookie watches the veteran lead the kids through a Bible story, deal with a discipline issue, or even observe how the schedule unfolds. Afterward, they debrief, and the more experienced teacher offers constructive feedback. Once or twice a year, all of the experienced and inexperienced teachers get together to share encouragements and best practices.

Alongside the year-long mentoring, veteran teachers can do one-time model teaching. Drew and Emily were married without children and volunteered in the four-year-olds' classroom. They were sweet and tried their best, but their lack of experience showed. Jennilee, a veteran teacher, demonstrated how to teach faithfully and in a developmentally appropriate way. As Drew and Emily watched Jennilee, lights went on. Once or twice, Drew excitedly said, "Oh, that's how you do it." What their teaching looked like after Jennilee's teaching session was drastically different than before.

The children's ministry team offers weekly reminders about policy—tidbits of information rather than a one-time, overwhelming training event. Every week, the childcare volunteers gather fifteen minutes before the classroom opens up to pray. Nathan, a children's ministry deacon, at the start of the meeting, offers a refresher. He'll remind those present of one small part of our child protection policy, such as, "Remember that only women can take preschool children to the restrooms," or "There must be at least two adults in every classroom," or "If a child hits another child, please pull the parents out of the worship service." Each time the volunteers gather, they get a bite-size portion of policy—something small enough to be easily digestible.

In addition to this on-the-job training, the children's ministry staff can host a big training event with lots of "carrots" to draw volunteers—host a banquet with delicious food, offer free gift cards to favorite stores. Be aware this won't be that much of a motivator. Some will come; plenty won't. But if you record this instruction, you can send a video or audio link and ask your folks to watch or listen to it at their convenience.

Other organizations can help with more specialized training. Last year I (Marty) hosted an ALICE (Alert, Lockdown, Inform, Counter, Evacuate) active shooter training for our ministry workers.[3] I took the instructor's training, which then equipped me to train our church leaders. To prepare for my class, ALICE provided each of our teachers and helpers with an online video training program. We both (Deepak and Marty) offered video training on recognizing and responding to child sexual abuse through an organization called Ministry Safe.[4] Even as larger churches, we don't have the resources to create our own specialized training but rely on reputable outside organizations to equip our folks.

Don't limit yourself. Think creatively about what training might fit your church context. And don't be afraid to think outside the box.

Retain, Nurture, and Protect

Patricia walked into a classroom. She'd never volunteered before. She had completed the initial volunteer training session, but she'd already forgotten much of what was said. She thought, *How hard could it be? We'll do some puzzles and read some books. Easy-peasy.* As she stepped into the two-year-olds' classroom, she was quickly overwhelmed. There were nineteen two-year-olds and only two other adult volunteers. The room was sheer chaos. Two other volunteers had called in sick, but supposedly more help was on the way. Kids were screaming constantly. She felt like she did nothing but change diapers the entire time. Little Johnny picked up a toy truck, threw it across the room, and wacked Cynthia in the head, leaving a bruise. An hour and a half later, Patricia walked out of the room, muttering under her breath, "I'll never do that again."

This was a real experience from a real person with an openness to children's ministry. But her good attitude vanished. Patricia left disappointed, frustrated, and disillusioned. Her bad experience in the classroom resulted in a Monday morning email to Ramona, the children's ministry director, saying she'd rather not volunteer again. Should it be any surprise? After a miserable experience, she won't come back.

A skeptic might argue, "Shouldn't Patricia have a stiff upper lip and put up with it? It's just two-year-olds, after all. What's the big deal?" Ramona should prepare Patricia for what's hard about children's ministry. No one can guarantee a classroom of two-year-olds will be easy to manage. But she should do what she can to make it a positive experience for the workers, especially the first few times they serve.

A gospel-rich, edifying experience makes a volunteer say, "I want more of that. I'd like to come back." Knowing it was Patricia's first time in the classroom, a visit from a coordinator halfway into the class would have gone a long way to encourage Patricia. We can't just set things up, send people into classrooms, and forget about them.

We've got to look at what's happening on the children's ministry floors, and if there are elements that automatically discourage the volunteers, Ramona does what she can to change it. The simple solution to the overwhelming childcare situation above was to break up the class into two rooms and add more adult volunteers to shift the ratio of adults to children.

Self-Evaluation: Do Your Volunteers Enjoy Children's Ministry?

Do your volunteers express the sentiment, "I'd like to serve again. Helping out children's ministry is encouraging!"? If not, what adjustments can you make to their service to help it be a positive experience (even though at times it can be hard)?

What expectations do you offer to our volunteers? Do your expectations accurately represent what they will face?

Offering proactive help

As volunteers gain classroom experience, they learn to ask for help when they need it. But Ramona should also be deliberate in asking them what they need.

As the volunteers become better at what they do, they take more responsibility over the course of time—rookies become lead teachers, teachers become coaches for the whole team, volunteers become deacons, and so on. Ramona cultivates an environment where the members own more of the ministry.

Ramona is humble enough to receive feedback. A part of the volunteer's ownership of the children's ministry is having a say in what does and doesn't work. Constructive feedback helps her make things better and helps the volunteers to feel heard.

Ramona shows gratitude for the volunteers. She doesn't take for granted that God has provided help for the little ones. She says "thank you" often, but goes above and beyond with cards, food, and fun field trips. She gets a stack of $5 gift cards to a local coffee shop and looks for folks who take initiative, do well with a difficult child or classroom, or demonstrate faithful and prompt attendance over time.

Protect the spiritual well-being of your volunteers

Children's ministry organizes itself typically around the needs of the children. Yet, if those needs are overwhelming, it can be too much for limited (and sometimes understaffed) volunteers. *The church's priority should be to protect the spiritual well-being of the volunteers.* The church's leaders shouldn't let folks serve so often that they get burned out. Instead, leaders should start with whatever framework is spiritually best for their volunteers and then organize the children's programs around those parameters. For example, in both of our churches, we've independently decided that a childcare worker can miss the main church service just once a month, but after that, they should be in the service with the rest of the congregation. Anything less would be detrimental to a volunteer's soul.

Let's suppose you've got lots of children in your program (e.g., fifty kids ages zero to ten) but few volunteers (e.g., eleven adults). In this situation, you can't safely staff the programs. You show your willingness to prioritize volunteers' spiritual well-being by closing a class for that Sunday or shutting down programs until you can adequately staff. "That's impossible," you say in response. "The parents will get angry and the pastors would get frustrated if we closed classrooms." The reality is, however, that a situation such as the one described above would be untenable over the long-term. Ask yourself—what would it take for us to shut down programs if needed? Have you built too big a children's program, one that is not sustainable? Do you need to reevaluate what you are doing?

Prioritizing your worker's spiritual well-being means asking them to take time off from serving. You want them to participate in the main worship service as a way to care for their soul. Sometimes a hurting couple whose marriage is on the rocks serves in children's ministry to get their minds off their troubles. It helps this couple to get their focus off of themselves and on to others (Philippians 2:3–4). But more often, a couple in a troubled marriage, a young adult hooked on pornography, or a burned-out single mother—they all need to sit undistracted in the worship service. For a season, they desperately need to sit under the weekly preaching, sing with the congregation, and pray along with the pastor. God's Word has answers for their troubles. Thus, we're prioritizing their hearing of the Word (Romans 10:17) and their spiritual growth (Colossians 1:27–28) during these difficult seasons. What matters most is a volunteer's soul, not a warm body to get the job done. Protecting members' long-term spiritual health will strengthen your children's ministry team in the long run.

The Father Knows What You Need

It's essential to keep our focus and trust in the Lord and not be overwhelmed with the day's needs. Do you need more workers for your ministry? Do you need to pause a program everyone loves because the leader moved to another church and you don't have someone to take over? Don't carry the weight of those challenges alone; take them to the Lord, while also remembering that it takes an entire church to make up a successful children's ministry. When encouraging the disciples to lift up their needs, Jesus told them, "your Father knows what you need before you ask him" (Matthew 6:8). What an encouraging reminder!

Early on, about two years into leading our children's ministry, I (Marty) was feeling overwhelmed. Our fledgling church plant was renting a community center. That required we turn adult daycare rooms into classrooms every Sunday and put everything back into a small storage room at the end of the day. Every Sunday, we rolled out carpets and pulled out the bins. I was exhausted and needed help.

I still remember the Sunday Dwayne came up to me and said, "You look like you need some help. Can I help you?" While Dwayne was doing the talking, it was God working for my good and the good of the ministry behind the scenes. The Lord prompted Dwayne's offer.

At that moment, all I was hoping for was extra hands to help load our bins and get me out of the building on time. But what I got was much, much more. Dwayne was not just offering to help load the cart; he volunteered to take over the entire administration of our ministry—and did so for the next eighteen years! Dwayne and his wife Tony had our children's ministry running like a well-oiled machine and gave up hundreds of hours of their time each year to serve the families in church for nearly two decades.

Now I know what you are going to ask, "How can I find a Dwayne and Tony?"

First, pray. God knows and can provide for everything we need. But second, remember your church is filled with everyday members who are gifted to serve. They raise families, lead small businesses, graduate with degrees in engineering, or babysit for large families. Trust the Lord; believe he's given you the adult members you need to care for the kids in your ministry. Serve faithfully, pray continually, and watch him work to provide everything you need.

7. Parents Build a Robust Partnership

The first Friday after his conversion, Terrance called his only Christian friend and asked, "What do Christians do on Friday night?" Previous to that, he and his girlfriend Ebony drank, bar hopped, and crashed parties. Ebony had moved in with Terrance while they dated.

Terrance met a Christian coworker and studied the Bible for a few months. In studying John's Gospel, he became a Christian. Terrance shared the gospel with Ebony, and she also believed. Shortly after their radical conversions, they married. Nine months later, their first child entered their life. As new parents, Terrance and Ebony imitated a lot of what they had learned from their own parents. The problem was—neither of them grew up in a Christian home.

During her first year, their daughter Kala had trouble sleeping and would often wake up in the middle of the night. By the age of three, Kala threw tantrums with the ferocity of an angry tiger. The day Kala turned seven, Ebony wondered if the Bible might help. "Terrance," she inquired one evening after tucking Kala in for the night, "should we be trying to teach Kala the Bible?"

All Terrance could think about was the big fat study Bible that sat on the living room coffee table. He had trouble enough trying to figure out what to read himself. He had read through the New Testament once. He tried reading the Old Testament but got lost once he hit Leviticus. He couldn't imagine reading Leviticus to Kala. "I think she's too young for the Bible," he replied to Ebony's question.

"I wonder if the Bible tells us what we should be doing?" Ebony asked. "Not that I've seen," Terrance answered. "If I remember, I'll ask Scott what he does with his kids."

A Spiritual Legacy to Future Generations

The Bible does have many things to say about parenting and passing a spiritual legacy on to our kids. Psalm 78 is an excellent place to start:

> Give ear, O my people, to my teaching;
> incline your ears to the words of my mouth. . . .
> We will not hide them from their children,
> but tell to the coming generation
> the glorious deeds of the Lord, and his might,
> and the wonders that he has done.
> He established a testimony in Jacob
> and appointed a law in Israel,
> which he commanded our fathers
> to teach to their children,
> that the next generation might know them,
> the children yet unborn,
> and arise and tell them to their children,
> so that they should set their hope in God
> and not forget the works of God,
> but keep his commandments;
> and that they should not be like their fathers,
> a stubborn and rebellious generation,
> a generation whose heart was not steadfast,
> whose spirit was not faithful to God. (Psalm 78:1, 4–8)

Psalm 78 is a psalm of Asaph. Asaph is one of three Levites commissioned by King David to be in charge of singing in the house of Yahweh. This psalm was probably a musical piece sung by the Israelites and used to remind the Israelites how God had been abundantly patient with them. Generation after generation gave in to unbelief and rebelled against the Lord. This psalm was a word of instruction from Asaph to the Israelites (v. 1).

Terrance and Ebony's goal (and really *any* Christian parent's goal) should be the same as Asaph's: to leave a spiritual legacy to future generations. "We will *not hide* them from their children, *but tell* to the coming generation the glorious deeds of the Lord, and his might, and the wonders that he has done" (v. 4, emphasis added).

Psalm 78 is a history lesson with a point—tell your children about the Lord and his glorious deeds. Don't ever hide what God has done. Pass these things down to the coming generation.

We want coming generations to know God, set their hope in him, and keep his commandments (vv. 6–7). Our greatest aspiration is not that our kids grow up successful, rich, and happy, but that they would know and love the Creator of the universe.

The warning throughout Psalm 78 is to "remember" and "not forget" (vv. 7, 11, 35, 42). If the Israelites were careless about teaching God's deeds, the next generation would fail to remember. Christians, by nature, are also forgetful; we need the same warning. We must tell our children so that they will one day "arise and tell . . . their children" (v. 6).

We are responsible for helping the parents in our ministry pass on the glorious deeds of the Lord to their children. Parents can sometimes wrongfully expect the children's ministry to take on the responsibility of training their kids about God, but it is clear from Asaph's charge that the whole of God's people joins in passing on our faith. "We will not hide them from their children" (v. 4). The prime responsibility for passing on the faith, however, does rest with the parents (v. 3).

So we partner with parents, who carry the primary responsibility. It means we pass on truth to their kids, but it also means helping them take the baton and run with it Monday through Saturday.

Trusting God and obeying him is not automatic for the next generation.[1] Each generation has its own choice—to trust in God and hold on to his promises or to turn away in unbelief. With every generation that chooses to believe, a spiritual legacy begins.

Though God has charged parents with passing on their faith, many are intimidated by this prospect. If Terrance were sitting across from us in our office, we'd hear him reluctantly explain, "I'm not a good teacher. I thought that's why we have pastors. I can't teach my kids." As an immature believer and a young Christian parent, his fear is evident. But teaching our children about God is not optional. It's a command. "He established a testimony in Jacob and appointed a law in Israel, which *he commanded* our fathers to teach to their children" (78:5, emphasis added). The stakes are high. If we fail to teach, our kids suffer because of our neglect—and not just our kids but future generations that follow.

God knew parents would need help passing the story of redemption on to our children. Consider the deliverance of Israel from Egypt. Their story unfolds with incredible twists and turns. God could have delivered the Israelites by sending the Egyptians into confusion. But God doesn't do that. Instead, the Lord sends ten plagues. Why the ten plagues? We get the answer in Exodus 10:2: "that you may tell in the hearing of your son and of your grandson how I have dealt harshly with the Egyptians and what signs I have done among them, that you may know that I am the Lord."

Go all the way back to the Exodus, and you see that God has future generations in mind. God's plan of redemption is a generational plan. He wrote a story for parents to tell their children and the many generations that follow. God doesn't have in mind just a single generation, but he is looking down the corridor of time toward future generations. That means he wrote the story for our kids too!

Parents tell God's story as a part of God's plan. Parents pass on their faith by telling their kids this story. Isn't it kind of

God to give parents something they can do to participate in the Lord's rescue plan?

Our job (as children's ministry staff or veteran Sunday school teachers) isn't babysitting; it's discipling. Just like parents, we get to pass on this story. We teach the kids this story on Sunday or Wednesday night, and then we help the parents teach the very same story the rest of the week.

Our job in children's ministry is not to just tell the same story but to come alongside parents to form a partnership. What might this look like?

A Gospel Partnership

We desire a strong and robust partnership between children's ministry and parents. Some Christian parents view the church as the place where their children can "get saved." These parents neglect to teach the Word at home, which puts more pressure on the church to produce Christian children. They send their kids to church, Christian schools, and camps, expecting that full-time Christian ministry folks will teach, instruct, and model faith for their kids. (One ornery parent once said, "After all, that's why we tithe, right? We pay you so you can do this work for us.")

There is no formula to produce Christian children, where we say the right things, do the right things, and out pops a born-again kid. There is no such thing. God must redeem our children. We know only God saves (Jonah 2:9). Yet, in his magnificent plan, he uses means to accomplish his sovereign purposes in salvation (Romans 10:14–15). God uses parents to point children to the truth and the gospel community around them to underscore the message of the gospel.

Children's ministry (and the church as a whole) is another means that God uses to declare his truth to the coming generations. Children come weekly to sit in Bible classes, listen to the prayers from the adults, and sit under the preaching of God's Word in the main worship service. God uses adults in church to point children to the truth.

Children's ministry should never replace Christian instruction in the home. We teach, model, and disciple children while they are at church a few hours a week. But we also (as a church) build up parents so they can fulfill what God asks them to do—teach the next generation about who he is and about his wondrous deeds (Psalm 78:4–5).

How does the church come alongside Christian parents to equip them in this task?

1. Spiritual maturity is always our first goal

This is what we expect of parents (and any member of our church):

- They attend the weekly worship services to join with others in prayer, sing, and sit under the preaching of God's Word.
- At least once a month, they partake of the Lord's Supper with the rest of the congregation.
- A parent meets for one-on-one Bible study and prayer with an older, faithful Christian from the same congregation. They are mentored and poured into.
- Parents engage in regular fellowship with other believers.
- They daily spend personal time in prayer and God's Word.

These are not optional add-ons for the Christian life. God uses these spiritual disciplines to grow parents in faith, hope, and love.

The best Christian parenting comes from a mom and dad firmly grounded in Christ. Maturity in Christ is the goal, not just for parenting, but for all of life. The apostle Paul declares,

> To them, God chose to make known how great among the Gentiles are the riches of the glory of this mystery, which is Christ in you, the hope of glory. Him we proclaim, warning everyone and teaching everyone with all

wisdom, *that we may present everyone mature in Christ.* (Colossians 1:27–28, emphasis added)

If parents are missing church services often (for whatever reason), if they are not plugged into a small group, if a mom or dad doesn't meet up with an older Christian to study the Bible, if they never spend any time in the Word or prayer on their own, then we're not moving towards this most important of goals.

2. We equip parents to know what Christian parenting looks like in the trenches of real life

You can't presume that parents will just "get it." If you didn't grow up in a Christian home, then you don't know what Christian parenting looks like. You don't know what it means (though you can try to make up for that with Christian videos and books). You *experientially* don't know what it's like and how biblical truths shape and define a home.

There is far too often a gospel deficit in our parenting. How many parents would be embarrassed if someone played a videotape of their parenting? What would we see? Ugly comments, screaming, impatience, and constant fighting? Parents can sometimes act like the Bible is irrelevant for what happens between Monday and Saturday. You may think the work of a children's ministry is limited to teaching the children. But the children are connected to families, and the family context is where they most grow and mature in their faith. So helping families is often the key to real growth in these children's lives.

The pastor can share parenting principles from the pulpit whenever it's appropriate to the text of the sermon. Staff can also instruct in parenting classes, offered for all age groups. An older father or mother in the faith can come alongside and mentor younger parents. There is an abundance of ways we can pass on truth and wisdom to younger parents.

Terrance sat in the car with Scott, his discipler, as Scott drove his son, Jacob, to soccer practice. In recounting the story to us, Scott couldn't remember what prompted Jacob's tantrum, but his four-year-old son had an all-out-scream-your-head-off fit. All the parenting books in the world can't teach Terrance what he witnessed over the next few moments—a father frustrated at first (that's Scott's sin), then calming down his son with gentle words, and patiently helping little Jacob to work through his tantrum. It's parenting in 3D—live, in person, real, and raw. Terrance, as a young believer, observed something that he never got growing up in a non-Christian home—a Christian parent whose gentleness (Proverbs 15:1), care, and patience (Ephesians 4:1–3; 6:4a) gives off the aroma of Christ.

3. We encourage parents to start with the Bible

We want to build into parents a desire and confidence to read the Bible and instruct their children. If the Bible is functionally irrelevant to what's going on in the home and parents have no personal engagement with Scripture in their lives, it won't show up in their interactions with the kids. If parents don't treasure God's Word as the very words of God himself, then the Bible will be absent from the home. However, if parents think, *This book contains the very words of eternal life*, they will do whatever it takes to make Scripture relevant to everything they do with their children.

Here are a few practical suggestions about a parent reading the Bible to his children.[2] Picture Jimmy, a dad, teaching his three kids—Benny, Betty and Peter.

He reads the entire Bible. When the kids are younger, he starts with the Old Testament and Gospel stories, sometimes taking time to retell stories in his own words. As they get older, he adds and explains more abstract portions of Scripture, like the Pauline epistles.

He reads thoughtfully. If Jimmy reads with a monotone voice, his kids quickly get bored. Instead, he reads in a way that makes the words comes to life. Sometimes he even uses different voices for different characters, or more inflection and more pronounced pronunciation of key words or ideas.

He points to Jesus.[3] Jesus is the new Adam; where Adam failed, Christ succeeded. Jimmy helps his kids make connections between the different parts of the Bible and Jesus. Moses, Joshua, and David all point forward to Christ.

He dialogues with his kids. Rather than turning it into a monologue, he asks questions to help his children engage with the stories and learn from them. "Why did God bring a flood?" (Genesis 6:11–13). "Why didn't the rich young ruler give up his wealth?" (Matthew 19:21–22). "Why did Jesus weep when he saw Mary and the crowds after Lazarus died?" (John 11:33–35).

They pray, sing, and memorize Scripture together. Jimmy models prayer. Don't be surprised if his kids start praying just like him, because they've heard him do it often. Jimmy and his kids sing truth and memorize it as another way to know Christ.

What can we do as a church to help these parents? We equip parents to understand how to read their Bible properly and how to share with their children. The kind of teaching Jimmy submits himself to in his local church will dictate how he teaches his children. If his pastor carefully explains the Bible text and applies it every time he opens the Bible, Jimmy learns from him how to read the Scriptures correctly. If an older man in the faith in one-on-one discipling works through books of the Bible with Jimmy, he learns how to read and ask questions of the text and how to apply it. And as parents learn these things, Jimmy grows more confident in his ability to do this with his children.

It's far too easy for parents to presume that much of the Bible will be beyond their children's comprehension. But that's just not true. We challenge parents to teach the rich and deep truths of Scripture in a developmentally appropriate way but to not water it down.

4. We equip parents with gospel tools

Books or curriculum should never replace a family's Bible reading, but there is an abundance of books, catechisms, curricula, and music that might help supplement our teaching. Because most Christian books or curricula are not available at your local public library, Christian parents and the church staff are a Christian resource library. Parents can highlight good books for other parents and pass them around. Church staff can also draw attention to resources and give them out on Sundays (see appendix D on pages 190-193 for a list of recommended resources).

Parents can expand a child's knowledge of faithful Christian living. He or she could read a biography about a Reformation character or a missionary. By reading biographies, parents offer living examples of the gospel to their children.

Parents could spend time at dinner reading about different countries in the world. It's good to expand the children's knowledge of God beyond the boundaries of their own neighborhood, to see how big and mighty the Lord truly is.

5. We help parents to endure in faith

Jimmy and his daughter Betty have a fight, and Jimmy spends the next hour feeling like a failure and wanting to give up. He piles self-condemnation onto the situation, mumbling to himself afterward, "You're an idiot of a parent" or "You're no better than your dysfunctional parents."

In parenting, you want to play the long game. You help parents remember that one nasty fight or lousy day doesn't have to set the tone for their home. Out of fear and a lack of faith, parents let hard days define them far too much, but it doesn't have to be so. The painful reality is that parents are going to sin and make mistakes.

There are two ways we set an example of faith in Christ for our kids. The first is obvious; children learn *by watching their parents obey and follow Jesus*. Parents show with their day-to-day choices what it looks like to trust Christ with all of their life. But what about the times when we sin? Second, parents set a good example *by demonstrating humble repentance*. When parents ask God for forgiveness, turn from their sin, and lean on Christ for strength, their kids have a front-row seat. God's grace teaches parents to live godly lives and steers us back to the cross when we fail. That is grace upon grace! These parents desperately need a heavy dose of God's grace.

The church holds out this grace to parents and reminds them again and again that their life is rooted in God's grace. Parents can endure and take hope as they stay grounded in the gospel.

Self-Examination: A gospel partnership

How is your church building up and supporting parents? What are you currently doing? What can you change, expand, or add to your current offerings?

Growing as Christian Parents

Kala got frustrated—she didn't want to eat what was on her plate. Terrance had been down this road with his daughter a dozen times before. Sometimes Terrance got frustrated with her. Other times he patiently instructed Kala that she couldn't have a fit and that she needed to finish what was on her plate.

Terrance and his discipler, Scott, talked about Terrance's impatience as a parent. Terrance didn't want to respond in this way. But there was hope. In and through Christ, Terrance grew to be more patient as he matured in his faith.

Terrance had grown as a Christian, and it spilled over into his parenting. Terrance now read the Bible at dinner time to Ebony and Kala. Initially, he thought, *I don't know how to do this*! But Terrance grew more comfortable and confident as he watched teachers in Sunday school do the same thing. After a few months of volunteering as a helper in Kala's Sunday school class, Terrance now thought, *With God's help, I can do this at home*.

It's an enormous privilege to come alongside parents and help them grow in greater faith and love. It's a privilege we share as we build partnership with parents, helping them to become all that Christ intends them to be.

A Note on Children's Ministry's Evangelistic Power

Our emphasis in the chapter is on the church discipling parents to fulfill their responsibility to teach their children the truths of our faith. But as a church, we have two other opportunities to keep in view.

First, the church serves an evangelistic role, sharing the gospel, perhaps for the first time, to children born into unbelieving households. They may show up for a VBS program or come along with a friend. We teach and model the gospel and pray for these children, just like we'd do with our own children.

Second, for all of our encouragement to parents, there will still be children in our ministries whose parents are Christians but are not providing consistent discipleship at home. When we are sharing the gospel consistently in our classrooms, we make up for the lack in homes that are not actively discipling their kids. While we can't take on the responsibility God gives parents, we can ensure any child entering our ministry is given the truth they need to come to know and love our Savior. Our opportunity to serve these children is much the same as for those from unbelieving households.

Part 3

The Practical Aspects of Children's Ministry

In part 1, we examined the *priorities* that build a sturdy foundation for our children's ministry. Teach the Bible. Value the children. Focus on the mission. These firm stones sit at the base of our tower, and on top of them, we'll construct a solid program.

In part 2, we described the Christ-honoring, faithful *people* who keep the ministry running. A part of God's wonderful plan is he uses people to accomplish the work of his kingdom. We (God's redeemed people) get the privilege of teaching and modeling truth for little children.

In part 3, we'll tackle the *practical* aspects of children's ministry. Too often we rush to the pragmatic aspects of ministry first, without building a proper foundation. But that's not what we've done. We've built our biblical foundation, recruited the right people, and now we're ready to consider the hands-on, concrete aspects children's ministry—things that must get done to make it all work.

Part 1 showed us *what we believe*, part 2 offered *who we rely on*, and part 3 will hold out *how we get these things done*.

Here's what we cover in this last section:

Keep Kids Safe. Sex abusers and predators target churches and other organizations that care for children. If we ignore this sad reality, our children will suffer the consequences. We can't assume that it won't happen to us. We must think, plan, and show vigilance to ward off potential abusers.

Establish an Emergency Response Plan. Are your children's ministry volunteers trained to respond to a real-life emergency? Are they prepared to evacuate children in case of a fire or safeguard them from an active shooter? We must educate our staff and volunteers on how to respond appropriately to different situations. Ad hoc responses to dire circumstances are not sufficient. We must consider in advance what needs to be done to adequately prepare for emergencies.

Manage the Classroom. We can't assume our volunteers know how to manage a children's ministry classroom. Parents who serve come with differing parenting approaches. Singles who volunteer to help may lack practical experience working with kids. Our job is to provide the guidelines, tools, and direction our volunteers need to manage energetic kids.

Pursue Creative Excellence. Our ministry identity, the decor of our space, and our presentation in the classroom work together to create a fun and engaging environment—or they don't. We can unintentionally make truth feel cold, dry, and unwelcome, but with a bit of creativity, we can deliver that same truth in a way that helps it come to life. Of course, we must never compromise the core truths of the faith, but neither should we dismiss the importance of adding creative elements to our children's ministry environment to make learning fun and engaging.

8. Keeping Kids Safe (Part 1)[1]

Karen had an encounter with evil. She was an innocent teenager in a hallway of a local megachurch, heading home after a youth event. On her way out, Karen ran into Sam, the building manager. Sam often showed kindness to Karen, stopping to talk with her and offering her candy every time he saw her. As an employee, he had a good reputation among the church, known as the man who would fix anything for anyone at anytime.

On this fateful day, when the two ran into each other, Sam invited Karen into an empty classroom, and she innocently followed. After they stepped into the classroom, Sam's demeanor changed. He pulled her behind a row of stacked chairs and forced her to have sex. No one else was around. Karen didn't know what to do, so she just gave in to Sam's demands.

Afterward, he threatened Karen. "Don't tell anyone, or else I'll come after you and kill you." She promised not to say anything, but she couldn't hide it because she cried the whole rest of the day.

Sam had a rap sheet. He'd hurt other children. The church had hired him because several friends commended him to the pastor, saying, "Sam can fix anything." However, no one bothered to check into his past. If they had, they would have seen his run-ins with the law and other churches. That was this church's failure.

Are you surprised? You shouldn't be. Some churches don't take the time to check on an employee's past, like running a criminal background check. Yet children suffer abuse because adults don't do their due diligence. The tragedy is that this was avoidable harm.

The first step in protecting our children is figuring out *who* is plotting evil against them. Let's consider two types of sexual predators who try to hurt our children.

Two Types of Predators

There are two types of sexual predators—the *power* predator and the *persuasion* predator.[2] Both wreak great havoc in the lives of their victims. Predators are problematic for the police, parents, and societies in which they live, but they have different ways of accomplishing their evil deeds.

The *power predator* takes a child by sheer force. He overtakes his victim by overpowering her and forcing her into captivity. You can think in terms of a child grabbed in a park or a schoolyard, dragged into a car, and driven off without the child having the strength or ability to stop the sexual offender.

Best-selling author and risk-assessment expert Gavin de Beker describes it this way: "The power predator charges like a bear, unmistakably committing to his attack. Because of this, he cannot easily retreat and say there was merely a misunderstanding. Accordingly, he strikes only when he feels certain he'll prevail."[3]

Almost twenty years ago, Jaycee Dugaard was a young girl on her way to the school bus when Philip Craig and his wife Nancy Garrido abducted her. Nancy had scouted out Jaycee's path to school, and then one morning, just as Jaycee started walking down the road, the couple drove alongside her. Philip pulled out a stun gun, shocked the girl, and then Nancy pulled her into the back of the car. Philip would later say to his wife, "I can't believe we got away with this."[4] For many years after her abduction, Jaycee was a sex slave, locked up in a shed in the back yard of Philip and Nancy's home. In just one fleeting moment, Jaycee was robbed of her life and childhood innocence. Enduring several years of rape is a nightmare scenario, but Jaycee stayed alive and eventually escaped.[5] Unlike Jaycee, a power predator's victims are usually never heard from again.

The *persuasion predator* uses his warm personality and charm to convince others that he is trustworthy and kind. He does this to gain access to children. Then when the surrounding adults have let down their guard, this abuser hurts innocent children. That's exactly what Sam did to Karen. Think in terms of a wolf in sheep's clothing. The wolf intends to harm others but doesn't want you to discover his plans. So, he puts on the appearance of an innocent sheep to deceive you.

In church settings, we can mitigate the danger of power predators with a good structural setup in our children's ministry (a check-in desk, half-doors on classrooms, hall monitors, and a security check-in system). This does a lot to keep the power predator at bay. But a persuasion predator is far more of a concern because the predator's duplicity allows him to potentially infiltrate your setting and gain access to children.

The Myth of Stranger Danger

One of the most common myths about sex offenders is that they will be strangers who take away your child. Power predators do exist. They scope out playgrounds or other places with kids to abduct children and steal their lives. But in a church setting, our problem is much less often going to be with a stranger and much more often going to be with those whose lives regularly intersect with ours: fellow church attenders, childcare workers, family members, and neighbors. It's the people we know who pose a threat, not the people we don't know.

According to a US Department of Justice (DOJ) report, law enforcement statistics show that nine out of ten teen sexual abuse victims know their abuser. Acquaintances and family members victimize a far more significant number of young children compared to strangers. The DOJ study reports that 96.9 percent of child sexual abuse victims, five years old and under, are known to their abusers. Only 3.1 percent are strangers.[6] That means the children in your ministry are at far greater risk of abuse by their teachers, family members, and other children than strangers.

Many children are taught from an early age not to talk to strangers. But the bigger problem is those who live among us. Teaching our children to be wary of strangers can give a false sense of security. What parents often ignore is the familiar adult who is too friendly with our kids. Consider the following:

- Most abuse takes place within the context of an ongoing relationship.
- In most cases, strangers will become "friends" before they abuse.
- Some child abusers are married and abuse their own children.[7]

Most children know how to respond to an unwelcome stranger, but they're uncertain what to do when a "safe" adult makes them uncomfortable.

A Typical Profile for a Sexual Predator

Pretend you're taking a multiple-choice test. Take a look at the list below and make your best guess at who you think fits the profile of a sexual offender.

A. A young, single male architect

B. A "soccer mom" with four children

C. A pediatrician

D. A Catholic priest

E. A public schoolteacher

F. None of the above

G. A and D only

H. All of the above

The correct answer is "H." While sexual predators are statistically most often male, we can't assume this to be the only type of predator. There are some instances when women get trapped in this perverse sin. Most commonly, one thinks of a schoolteacher who leads teenage boys astray with inappropriate sexual encounters. But there are other categories of female offenders, including some with sadistic tendencies and those who are coerced by a male partner to abuse children.[8]

In fact, predators come in all types—single and married, blue collar and white collar, educated and uneducated, rich, middle class, and poor. In examining a range of sexual offender cases, we've found examples in almost every category of work—college professor, athletic director of a private school, Catholic priest, doctor, lawyer, pastor, and many other professionals. We can't limit sexual offenders to just one generic profile.

The Techniques of Predators

Questions abound when it comes to understanding sexual offenders. How do predators get away with the things that they do? How do they fool the church community and then the child? What methods do they employ to keep children from disclosing their grotesque behavior? If we understand a predator's techniques, it helps us to recognize potential problems *before* any harm comes to our children.

Grooming the church community

The most common technique for sexual offenders to gain access to children is to cultivate a double life. Sexual offenders work hard to be likable and respectable members of a church. If they are liked and respected, they earn the trust of the church community. Once they are trusted, they gain access to children. This process is known as "grooming"—a method of working over the children and adults in a church to earn their trust.

Offenders don't usually rush through grooming but instead take their time to develop relationships with the members of a church community. In order to win over the adults and become an accepted part of the church, they put on a persona of being useful, kind, helpful, polite, and caring to adults and children alike. Expert Anna Salter comments,

> The double life is a powerful tactic: There is the pattern of socially responsible behavior in public that causes parents and others to drop their guard, to allow access to children, and to turn a deaf ear to disclosures. But a surly and obnoxious person would have little access, no matter how proper and appropriate his public behavior was. The second tactic—the ability to charm, to be likeable, to radiate sincerity and truthfulness—is crucial to gaining access to children.[9]

Most violent offenders keep their behavior in check publicly so as not to draw suspicion. The fact that a sexual offender is not off-putting but might have good qualities makes it difficult to pinpoint one. Most people think of a sexual offender as all bad. They can't conceive of such a person having anything good about him or her.

Once the sexual predator has gained the trust of a significant number of people within a church, suspicions become harder to articulate. Conformity studies show that few people will publicly disagree with a majority opinion. And if the person gets enthusiastic support from church friends or church leaders, it makes it all the more difficult to speak out against him with persuasive conviction.

In reality, what often happens is that the sexual offender pretends to be someone he or she is not. Offenders are professional liars—they are skillful at what they do because they've done it for years. They've lied to everyone in their lives—church members, friends, their victims, and even to themselves—to justify their sinful desires and continue on the destructive path of harming children. According to most experts who work with sexual offenders, not only is their lying hard to detect, but it is often quite convincing.[10]

If a predator is roaming around your church, he is probably not a stranger to you. More than likely, he is someone you already know, like, and do not see as a threat to your children.

Grooming the child

Once a predator has earned the trust of a church community and perhaps of a particular family, gaining access to children in the process, he will start grooming a child. He will give gifts, words of praise, an extraordinary amount of attention, and show affection to the unsuspecting child. One sexual offender described his strategy this way: "When a person like myself wants to obtain a child, you don't just go up and get the child and sexually molest the child. There's a process of obtaining the child's friendship and, in my case, also obtaining the family's friendship and their trust. When you get their trust, that's when the child becomes vulnerable, and you can molest the child."[11]

In a church setting, you should watch out for a teacher or children's ministry volunteer who repeatedly brings special gifts for one child, who overtly bonds with this kid, or who gains access to this child outside of the church.

Regarding physical contact, the grooming of a child occurs across a continuum, starting with more innocent behaviors like touching an arm or tickling games, and then gradually moves to more risky behavior like kissing on the lips instead of the cheek, sexual jokes, or extended touch. The sexual predator's goal is to blur the lines between appropriate and inappropriate behavior, which opens the doorway to taking greater risks. Things progress with the child becoming more comfortable with each step, as an increasing level of sexuality is introduced into the relationship.[12]

In the grooming process, predators spend an unusual amount of time with kids. They engage children in behavior and play appropriate for the child's age and prefer to spend more time with children than adults. This behavior should lead observing adults to wonder why this person (an adult or even a teenager) would rather hang out more with young kids than their own peers.

Many sexual offenders are deliberate and careful in their planning. According to prosecutor and expert Victor Vieth, "sex offenders often look for the easiest target."[13] A prime example is a sexual predator who purposefully pursues more vulnerable children, such as kids with single or divorced parents. Think about what's happening in these families—the child often longs for a father figure, so he or she quickly gravitates toward any type of paternal influence. The single mother is exhausted and desperately needs help, so she all too quickly gives over the care of her kids to an interested adult to get a break. The predator's offer to help seems an answer to prayer, something to be celebrated, not investigated. Checking his or her references feels unthinkable and accusatory.

What other types of vulnerable children might sexual predators target? Offenders will prey on children who are experiencing family problems; children who are often in trouble; kids who are eager to please, who are picked on by other children, who are quiet, withdrawn, and isolated; kids who are disabled in some way that might make them less believable (e.g., cognitively disabled children); or kids who are too young to articulate the experience of abuse. Note what sex offender John Henry said in his testimony before the US Senate: "I showed them affection and the attention they thought they were not getting anywhere else. *Almost without exception, every child I have molested was lonely and longing for attention.* . . . Their desire to be loved, their trust of adults, their normal sexual playfulness and their inquisitive minds made them perfect victims."[14]

While all of our children can be abused, we need especially to keep a watchful eye on the most vulnerable and fragile children among us.

Counting on no disclosure

Children who are molested and disclose this to an adult are rarely taken seriously because their perpetrators seem unlikely to be sexual offenders. If your child said his teacher, doctor, or coach molested him, would you immediately believe him? Most of us want to say, "Yes, of course, we would." Yet, in reality, many parents would struggle with discerning between the folly of a child (Proverbs 22:15) and the reputation of a highly respected, well-known figure in the community.

Only a small minority of children will disclose abuse at the time it is occurring. If they do share, they may not disclose the most embarrassing details. Not surprisingly, sexual predators concerned about children disclosing (some are, some are not) will try to convince the child to keep it a secret. The following is taken from a "Q-and-A session" with a sexual offender:

> *Question*: How do you keep your victims from telling?
>
> *Answer*: Well, first of all, I've won all their trust. They think I'm the greatest thing that ever lived. Their families think I'm the greatest thing that ever lived. Because I'm so nice to them and I'm so kind and so—there's just nobody better to that person than me. If it came down to, you know . . . "I have a little secret, this is our little secret," then it would come down to that, but it doesn't have to usually come down to that. It's almost an unspoken understanding.[15]

Sadly, children are too often ignored, which in turn increases the sexual offender's confidence level and his willingness to take risks. A dreadful consequence of children keeping secrets or adults not believing them is that most offenders will end up with dozens of victims before they are ever caught.[16]

What Should You Do?

We'll recommend a host of best practices on preventing abuse in the next chapter, but here we conclude by offering thoughts on what to do with this difficult information about sexual offenders.

Be careful of your assumptions. Do not assume you know who is and who is not a sexual offender. Most people falsely think they can identify a predator—he or she would be a "monster." Maybe he's a single man? Someone who is disheveled? Maybe he has some kind of evident mental illness or addiction or insanity? He probably is uneducated or some sort of pervert. If you think this way, then predators already have you fooled. Carefully examine your assumptions to make sure you have accurate information about sexual predators.

Teach your volunteers about grooming. Your church members reside at the front lines of the day-to-day work of children's ministry. Give them tools to recognize the techniques of a sexual predator. The more your members know, the more likely they'll sound the alarm and call out abuse when it happens or when they suspect something is amiss.

Post your policies. Create a written child protection policy and require all parents and workers to read the policy. Post signs that will make predators think twice about abusing your children. Signs with wording such as, "Children must be accompanied by more than one adult" on your children's ministry bathroom doors underscores expected behavior. If you have cameras, post a sign that says, "Children's ministry is under video surveillance."

Train the gatekeepers. Every church community has gatekeepers—people who make the final decision about volunteers and access to children. A predator grooms the whole community, but he's chiefly concerned about deceiving the gatekeepers.[17] If a sexual predator convinces the gatekeepers that he's trustworthy and kind, he'll get what he wants—time with church children. That's why the gatekeepers must have a higher, more sophisticated level of training compared to all the rest of the church. A few suggestions for gatekeeper training: (1) Read Deepak's book *On Guard: Preventing and Responding to Child Abuse at Church*,[18] and (2) take your church's leadership and children's ministry team through *Ministry Safe*'s training.[19]

Keep a healthy level of skepticism. We can't make naïve assumptions about how sexual offenders operate. A healthy skepticism recognizes that we live in a fallen world where people do evil things against children. For example, if a young single man (let's call him "Steve") takes a child to the restroom by himself, it should raise yellow flags for us. The church policy states children must be accompanied to the bathroom by a woman volunteer, not a man. If Steve, as an inexperienced single guy, watched Ronald (a four-year-old) scream, "I'VE GOT TO GO WEE-WEE!" Steve will rush Ronald to the restroom to avoid an accident. He's not thinking carefully about the bathroom policy. But what if this is not a one-time incident? What if Steve takes little boys to the restroom a few times, in violation of the policy? Then there *is* reason for concern. If a volunteer notices Steve's policy violations, he or she must speak up. A healthy skepticism wouldn't rush to judgment, but it would take steps to call out the policy violation and learn what's truly going on. Maybe Steve is clueless, or maybe he's doing something malicious. Either way, this situation can't be left alone or brushed under the rug.

Teach your kids to say "no." Because of the myth of stranger danger, it's important to teach children to say "no" whenever an adult crosses an inappropriate boundary. Tell your kids that no one (apart from mommy or daddy or a doctor or nurse) is allowed to see the parts of their body covered by a bathing suit. It only takes thirty seconds for a child's life to be ruined, so get out ahead of the sexual offender and teach your kids to say "no." *God Made All of Me* by Justin and Lindsey Holcomb is a book written to help caregivers teach children on this topic and is a helpful resource you can recommend to your parents.

Always report. Don't wait until an investigation proves an allegation correct. If you suspect abuse could be occurring, report your suspicions to the authorities and allow them to investigate.

Keep Kids Safe

As Christians, we must protect the children whom God has entrusted to us. We have an ethical and moral responsibility to do so. Children are a heritage and a reward from God (Psalm 127:3). Whoever dares to harm them should heed Jesus's warning: "If anyone causes one of these little ones—those who believe in me—to stumble, it would be better for them if a large millstone were hung around their neck and they were thrown into the sea" (Mark 9:42 NIV).

You might read this chapter and think, *Oh, my. This whole thing is scary*, and you walk away worried about the threat of a predator. Lord willing, you are now better equipped to understand this problem of abusers.

If you're walking away feeling more concerned that a child abuser might harm your children, that's probably a good thing. The realities of child abuse are deeply disturbing, and they should motivate us to take seriously the protection of children in our churches. However, far be it from us to end this on a note of fear. As Christians, we live not in fear, but in confidence in the God of grace.

As followers of Christ, where does our hope finally come from? Not in anything we can do in this world but in the God of grace who equips us to walk in his wisdom and strength. As believers, we must not live in fear but with confidence and trust in the Lord. We should serve our children and our churches with the same confidence King David wrote about as he faced trials and difficulties:

> When I am afraid, I put my trust in you.
> In God, whose word I praise—
> in God I trust and am not afraid.
> What can mere mortals do to me?
> (Psalm 56:3–4 NIV)

Self-evaluation: keep kids safe

What is your church doing to prevent child abuse? Do you have your child protection policies written down? Do you conduct regular training? If you are not doing anything by way of child protection, where can you start?

9. Keeping Kids Safe (Part 2)

Jonathan was sick to his stomach. No pastor ever wants a child hurt. Yet his church faced a lawsuit over sexual abuse that recently occurred in their children's ministry. He was bogged down with conversations with a lawyer, seeking to shepherd the distraught families in his congregation, feeling guilt over his failed leadership, and trying to hold things together. According to Jonathan, "It felt like a bomb just went off, and I'm cleaning up the mess."

Clarence was a friendly man who had joined First Baptist Church about a year ago. He was kind and the members of First Baptist took a quick liking to him. He volunteered to teach a Sunday school class and got to know Peter, an eight-year-old boy in his class. Things started innocently. A hug at the end of class. Gifts for Peter. Lots of extra attention.

And then it happened. Clarence took advantage of Peter. He made Peter keep it a secret. But Peter became apathetic, withdrawn, and passive (which was not like him), and his mother Nicolle grew concerned. Eventually, Peter told his mother about the abuse, and she was horrified.

Nicolle contacted the pastor immediately, but the church failed to report the incident. Jonathan, the senior pastor, didn't want to rush to judgment. He allowed Clarence to attend services that next Sunday. Sadly, Jonathan's attitude towards the abuse made the situation much worse. Nicolle was outraged. "If that pastor and the church are not going to do anything, then they leave me with no choice." She contacted the police, then later hired an attorney and filed a suit against the church.

When Churches Fail our Kids

Sadly, this is an all-too-familiar story. If you pay any attention to the news, you are well aware that sexual offenders show up in churches. Like predators hurting defenseless prey, they do unspeakably horrible things to our children. Much of what is done could be prevented, but too many churches are ignorant about how to protect children and how to appropriately respond when sex abuse happens at church. It adds up to being irresponsible with the little ones that God has entrusted to our care.

Why do churches fail our kids?

- Because churches are desperate for volunteers, sexual offenders know they can get easy access to kids.
- Because churches tend to be more informal than childcare centers, they often don't bother checking on someone's past or screening volunteers.
- Because church members may make too many assumptions about sexual abuse, they may think things like, *It will never happen to us*, or *We know everyone at church and none of our friends would do something like this*.
- Because church members may make too many assumptions about sexual offenders, they may assume they are not anything like us, when in fact, sexual offenders come in all types—white collar or blue collar, single or married, male or female, educated or uneducated, rich or poor.
- Because church members may get offended when the children's ministry director starts implementing protective measures (e.g., requiring applications and screening members before they can volunteer). Longstanding members think, *How dare you ask me? I've*

been here for twenty years. Or others think, *We're a small church. We're like a family. Why do we need this?*

- Because sexual offenders are smart, they know Christians can sometimes be naïve, so they take advantage of their trust. Some will cultivate a double life, appearing like the nicest guy in the world. They do this to get easy access to children.
- Because when child sex abuse happens at church, there are often no policies in place to address it. When pastors try to handle this internally without a response plan and without involving authorities, children are victimized yet again—but this time by church authorities.
- Because churches misapply the scriptural call to forgive in ways that can press for reconciliation between victims and their abusers. This response, coupled with a desire to "move on," results in a lack of adequate care for victims and their families.

Many more reasons can be listed, but these give you a sense of what could go wrong.

Best Practices for Protecting Against Child Abuse

What can be done about this problem? How can pastors and churches be more responsible in protecting our children? Let's consider a few best practices. None of these strategies by themselves can eliminate the possibility of a sexual offender hurting your church kids. But together they can reduce the risk and increase the likelihood that our kids will be safe.

1. Create and implement a child protection policy

A child protection policy (CPP) is a set of self-imposed guidelines that describe how a church creates a safe environment for the children. When carefully written and thoughtfully taught and implemented, the church uses the CPP to protect the children under its care. The main point of children's ministry is not just to teach truth to kids (though this is important!) or provide adequate childcare. We also want to facilitate the parents' participation in the church services without the parents worrying about their children's protection and care.

If a church's ministry to the kids is ad hoc and not well planned out, the kids and the parents will suffer. Policies should be written, clear, uniform, distributed to staff to study, and reviewed annually. A church with no written policy is a recipe for disaster because it creates a culture of false assumptions that sexual offenders prey on, such as, "We are a small church so we know everyone."

Two general principles typically undergird a CPP. First, *the risk of abuse increases when a child is isolated with an adult.*[1] Many offenders look for privacy in order to commit abuse, so we try to ensure an adult is never isolated with children.

Second, *the risk of abuse increases as accountability decreases.* If an adult is alone with a child, there is no accountability from another adult. Or if a children's event occurs without any knowledge of the leadership or the staff, then there is not accountability from the church as a whole.

Both principles help your church assess the level of risk in a situation and implement policies that make children's ministry a safe place for kids.[2] Risk-lowering factors will include

- increasing the number of adults present and requiring more than one adult to be present with children at all times
- hosting children's ministry activities on church property rather than a private home and hosting at a time when more people will be around
- increasing the visibility of adults and children
- organizing the setup such that there are clear physical boundaries that "fence in" childcare workers and children and keep out everyone else
- cultivating a personal knowledge of the character and integrity of the staff or volunteers

- ensuring that staff and volunteers have participated in the church's training and screening procedures (including a background check and references)
- fostering a high degree of openness about children's ministry classes and events
- requiring approval of children's ministry activities by church leadership or staff

We cannot eradicate abuse from this world, but we can be deliberate in taking steps that lower the risk.

What policies and procedures should be included in a CPP? For an overview, see appendix B on page 178 ("Guide to Writing and Implementing a Child Protection Policy").

2. Utilize a check-in and check-out process

Clearly defined check-in and check-out procedures create a "fence" around the children, allowing them to reside safely in the care of the church until they are returned to their parents.

Consider two goals for this process. First, a check-in and check-out process clarifies when the child is under the care of the church volunteers or his parents. When a parent checks his son in and hands him over to the Sunday school teacher, that moment marks the point at which the church's children's ministry officially takes responsibility for that child. When is the child no longer the responsibility of the children's ministry staff and volunteers? After the parent checks the child out and receives the child back into his or her care. Without a clear check-in process, the line of responsibility becomes fuzzy. For liability's sake alone, it is good to make this line as distinct as possible.

Second, a check-in and check-out process gives volunteers an organized system that matches children with parents and vice versa. For example, you could use a system of numbered wrist bracelets, where one bracelet goes on each child's arm and a matching bracelet goes to the child's parent. If a volunteer was not sure if he was giving the right child to the correct parent, the check-out system would provide a way of ensuring he wasn't doing something wrong.

A check-in and check-out process signals to potential abusers who visit your church that your ministry is well organized and not easily accessed.

3. Make use of a thoughtful membership process

A big front door to your church is obvious to sexual offenders. Membership is a self-conscious commitment to the congregation that allows the church to define who is "in" and who is "out." Having no membership process (or a very minimal process) means people too easily flow in and out of the congregation without any clear definition of who is part of the church. Think for a moment. Where do you think a sexual offender will go—a church with a ten-week membership class plus an interview, or a church where you can join right away without any questions? The lower the membership hurdle, the more likely they will jump over it.[3]

4. Employ screening and verification procedures for staff and volunteers

Most sexual offenders assume you won't check up on them because most churches don't do any form of background check. Thus, another important step in protecting against predators is implementing screening and verification procedures for both staff and volunteers. These procedures will detect when sexual offenders are prowling around your church. Do not assume that because a volunteer is a self-professing Christian, he or she is okay to be with your kids. Ask about their backgrounds and employ professional screening services. This helps to verify that there are no skeletons in the closet.

As more is known about the recidivism of sexual predators, screening and background checks have become the standard of care. Should an incident occur in your congregation involving an unscreened adult who was given access to children, you may be liable for negligence, not to mention the avoidable harm inflicted on children.

In order to have an effective screening and verification process, a church will consider a number of tools to screen children's workers, including a written application, references, interview, background check, and possibly fingerprinting. A successful screening and verification program depends on employing a multifaceted approach, and not just one of these means.[4] Your goal is to verify that there are no skeletons in a person's closet and no criminal behavior in his or her past.

A criminal background check has become the standard of care for any organization that works with children. But a background check alone is not an effective means of screening. Why is that?[5]

- Less than 10 percent of sex offenders will have criminal records to check.
- Teen abusers have no searchable criminal records because juvenile records are generally unavailable.
- Sex offenders often "plea down" in court to lesser offenses.

That's why you should conduct interviews, use screening questions, and check references. These additional items can help to verify that a person comes recommended and is fit for service.

5. Carefully consider your building design

Have you ever thought about how you can adjust your building design to guard against sexual offenders infiltrating your church? Building layout (and the structural setup of your children's ministry wing) may not be the most obvious strategy in dealing with sexual offenders. It's probably the thing you are least able to change in your church. Yet, there may be simple adjustments (or larger ones) that you can make to help the children in your church be more secure.

We have four goals for the design of the children's ministry area:

1. We want a *single access point* (entrance) to the children from the general church population.
2. We want *clear physical boundaries* that fence in the kids and approved volunteers and keep out those who should not have access to the kids.
3. We ensure that there are *no isolated areas* where an adult can be alone with a child.
4. We want *unobstructed visibility* into all of the classrooms.

The following three kinds of structural setups frequently characterize churches. These building designs below are especially for the youngest children (zero to five years of age) because they are the most vulnerable.

The Ideal Setup. This configuration uses walls to separate the entire children's ministry area from the rest of the church and a centralized check-in desk, which all volunteers and children must pass through. Anyone looking at this setup immediately gets the message: you are not getting in here without passing through check-in first.

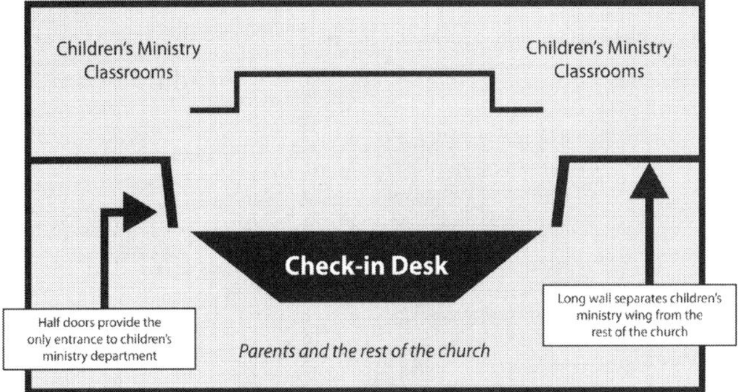

Eye Level

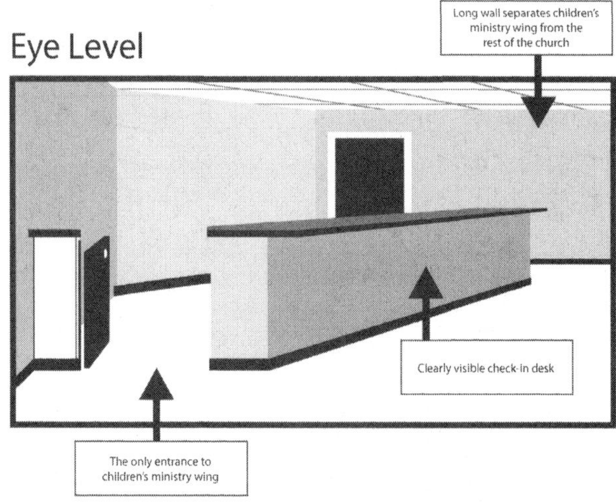

A Good Alternative. The next best option would be a long hallway with classrooms that are marked off with half-doors (e.g., Dutch doors) at the entrance to every classroom. The half-door option allows you to put a boundary between the parents in the hallway and the teachers and children in the classroom. It also provides considerable visibility if the top half of the door is left open.

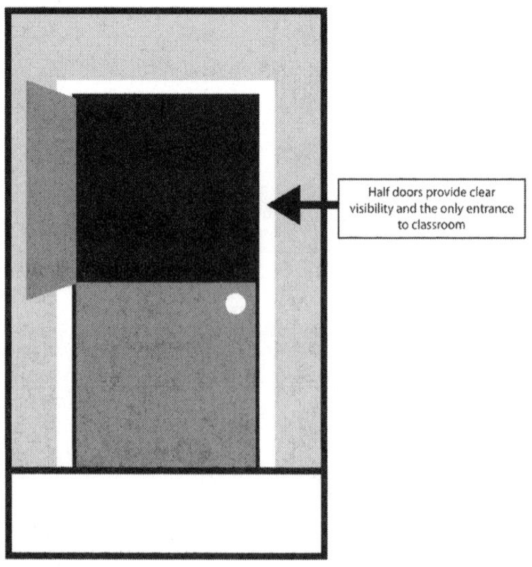

A Poor Configuration. The worst option is an unobstructed doorway where children (especially the youngest) or any adults can walk in or out, or a door that can be shut with no line of sight directly into the classroom. If you have no choice but to use a space like the one described above, consider using cameras to video monitor the hallways and classrooms. In fact, video surveillance can accentuate any of the above configurations and provide an additional deterrent against abusing a child in your ministry.

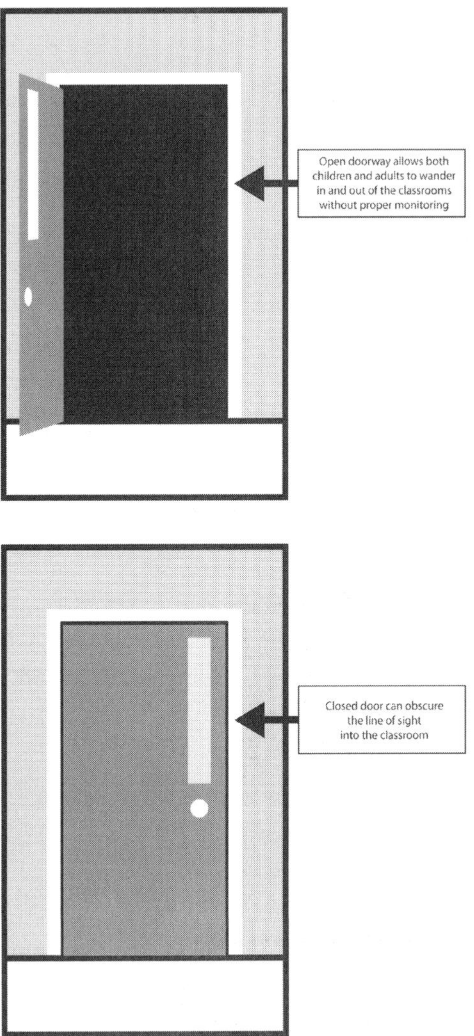
Open doorway allows both
children and adults to wander
in and out of the classrooms
without proper monitoring
Closed door can obscure
the line of sight
into the classroom

6. Train volunteers, staff, and church leaders

We can't allow volunteers to be haphazard or careless. Our objective is for every volunteer to be thoughtful, gospel-minded, and careful. It's our job to equip these volunteers with what they need to know.

Two types of training are important—entry-level training (for new volunteers) and ongoing training (for the veterans). We'll cover topics like a vision for children's ministry, evangelism, classroom expectations, policies and procedures, and of course, how to prevent and recognize child abuse and neglect. How do you answer the question, "What do our volunteers need to know to do their job faithfully, in a way that keeps children safe?"

Author and curriculum writer Connie Dever often says, "Preach good sermons and they will come. Run an excellent children's ministry, and they will stay." Protection of kids starts at the top. If the church leadership takes seriously this issue of child safety, then the church will see the difference. If the children's ministry is desperate for volunteers, or if the children's ministry director is faced with overwhelming resistance to these practices, often it is because the leadership is not supportive, or they just don't care.

We also take the time to equip church leaders and staff. Ignorance is tantamount to saying, "We're too busy to think about this." Bad information and careless assumptions about child abuse and neglect lead to bad decisions when things go wrong. We take steps to train leaders who are willing to listen and learn.

7. Proactively think through response plans

If a sexual offender arrived in the building, would your staff and volunteers know what to do? If a child was abused in your children's ministry, do you know how you would handle the offender? Do you know how to care for the victim and the victim's family? Do you understand the regulations for reporting abuse in your state? Do you know what to say to the media requests?

Response plans are crucial because they provide a set of procedures that guide the church's response to child abuse or the unexpected arrival of a sexual offender in your church services. A church with a response plan shows the leadership and staff have proactively thought about these things. If there are no plans in place, the pastor improvises when something terrible happens. He shows how unprepared he was for this difficult moment. Which church would you prefer to bring your kids to—the well-planned children's ministry or the fly-by-the-seat-of-your-pants approach?

8. Get to know your community

Get to know the resources in your community before a problem occurs. Find good doctors and counselors. Take a local Child Protective Services worker out to lunch so that when the time comes, you can make a phone call to someone you know rather than an anonymous call to a hotline. Make sure you know the best resources and personnel in your community so you can contact them if it is ever needed.

9. Equip parents

In November 2011, all of the major news networks covered the breaking story about former Penn State defensive coordinator Jerry Sandusky, who was accused of sexually abusing at least eight boys over a span of fifteen years. A lengthy grand jury investigation in 2010 and 2011 led to the arrest—as well a black mark on one of college football's most revered programs. In June of 2012, Sandusky was found guilty and given a thirty-year prison sentence.

In the wake of that scandal, our parents wondered what they could do to protect their children from similar crimes. For weeks after the Jerry Sandusky trial, we were regularly approached by parents who asked, "How do we speak about sexual abuse to our kids?" Here are some examples of what we did to help out our parents:

- We trained parents to take seriously their responsibility to be the primary disciplers of their kids. We encouraged them to be deeply invested in their children's lives, so predators couldn't hold secrets with their kids.
- We instructed parents to not avoid conversations about sex but to talk openly with their kids in age-appropriate ways. Parents can create a home environment that allows their kids to ask honest questions.
- We reminded fathers and mothers about the importance of instructing children on decorum, modesty, and respectful boundaries with other kids.
- We equipped parents to talk with their children about what to do if a Sunday school teacher or neighbor or relative tries to cross a forbidden line.
- We encouraged reporting all cases of suspected abuse to authorities. We reinforced the importance of reporting *suspected* abuse rather than "believing the best."

These are a few samples of what we did. The point being, don't leave your parents to figure this out on your own. Help them to know how to keep their kids safe and how to prevent abuse.

10. Get a review of your ministry

Once you've implemented a child protection program, invite someone from outside your church to access and review your policies and procedures. You can partner with another church that is working through these same issues. Invite their children's pastor or children's ministry director to look over your plan and suggest ways to improve. While hiring a professional to look over your policies can be costly, it is a wise use of funds. It can help protect your children and costs far less than the expenses of a negligence lawsuit against your church.

Adopt Best Practices for the Glory of Christ and the Honor of His Name

Pay attention to the news and you'll encounter far too many abuse cases in churches. Ignorance and carelessness lead to trouble. Sadly, much of this mayhem could have been prevented.

What do we want? We hope to be faithful stewards of the children entrusted to our care. We protect our kids, first and foremost, because we love them. Abuse is evil, and we must do everything in our power to stop it.

But we also want to preserve the gospel witness of our churches. We don't want our witness to be tainted by accounts of abuse. We don't want to be known as "that church," where abuse happened to the children; or "that church," who mishandled cases of abuse; or "that church," where the leadership did an internal investigation and didn't involve professional criminal investigators. This reckless behavior hurts the name of Christ.

We employ best practices because we want to honor Christ. We don't want his name to be dragged through the mud. We bring glory to his name by being faithful with all that he's asked us to do in children's ministry, including protecting our children and preventing abuse.

Word of Warning: Some children's ministry directors stress over their inability to implement all of these practices, especially if their church is small, has few resources, and is still overall unhealthy. Remember, the goal is to do as much as you can to reduce the risk. Not every church will be ready to employ all of these best practices at once. Make a plan for what you'd like to do, do everything you can, and pray about all the rest!

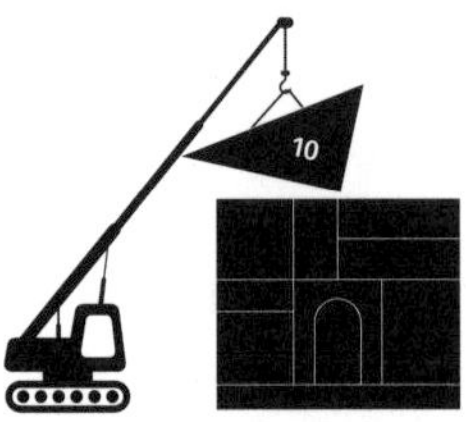

10. Establish an Emergency Response Plan

Brian, a father of twins, stopped by my (Deepak's) office on a Monday morning. After exchanging a few pleasantries, he asked, "Our children's school practiced a fire evacuation last week. Do you feel we're ready if a fire happened at our church?"

I was dumbfounded. For a moment, I imagined a fire blazing through the building and how ill prepared we would be. Kids might die because of our lack of preparation. Disastrous. Who wants that?

Shortly after Brian walked out, I called our children's ministry director and asked her questions about a fire evacuation. What began as a question from a thoughtful father ended a few months later with new signs on the walls, a new fire evacuation policy, new equipment, and a new once-a-year fire evacuation drill.

Emergencies will happen. We expect that in a fallen world. Fires, active shooters, tornadoes, hurricanes, earthquakes, and even bomb threats—you name it, and we can find a church that has faced it. You can operate as if you'll be the lucky ones—"These disasters are so unlikely, it probably won't ever happen to us," but to make that assumption is a recipe for trouble.

The goal of this chapter is to get you to consider emergency planning. Are you ready for when disaster strikes?

Be Prepared

Sheila read an ABC book to a couple of three-year-olds. Jeremy played with two boys building a house with wooden blocks. A moment later, someone screams, "FIRE! EVERYONE GET OUT!!"

Sheila and Jeremy are responsible for this group of rowdy three-year-olds. What you see next reveals if they were adequately trained for this moment. Consider two options.

Option A. They panic and shout directions at the kids. Maybe Jeremy bellows, "I've got them," and then grabs two boys in his arms and runs out the door. Sheila leads three other children out the door, and they run down the nearest staircase. No one ever told Sheila and Jeremy what to do, so they responded as best they knew how in the moment.

Option B. Sheila and Jeremy—with some anxiety, but mostly calm—get the kids together into a line, conduct a headcount, and then lead the children in an orderly way along an assigned route and out to a designated waiting area outside of the church building. They default to their training from a recent fire drill, and even though they forgot some elements, there were staff on hand and enough signs on the wall to remind them what to do.

Think for a moment—which option would better describe how your volunteers would respond?

Be prepared for emergencies before they strike. Plan and look for ways to prevent potential problems. Don't let disaster strike and catch you flat-footed. Get out ahead of it and nip it in the bud. Don't think through policy and procedures only *after* an emergency wreaks havoc.

Consider a few principles as you prepare for *any* kind of emergency:

- *Get training and talk to experts in the field.* Law enforcement, fire marshals, firefighters, and emergency response planners for the Federal Emergency Management Agency (FEMA) are experts at what they do. They know more than you on this topic, so take a class or consult with them (especially if a few are a part of your congregation).

- *Purchase equipment and outfit the children's ministry area.* Get baby carriers that hospitals use in case of fire. Purchase rope with tie loops for preschool kids to hold onto during evacuations. Put locks on the inside of the doors in case you need to lock down an entire floor to prevent a shooter from entering, and place first-aid kits in classrooms in case of a medical incident (like a child getting a cut). Then follow up with periodic inspections to make sure your equipment stays suitable for regular use. For example, keep fire extinguishers up to date and tested, ensure batteries are fresh in your smoke and CO2 detectors, and make sure first-aid kits are properly stocked with supplies.
- *Write out a policy.* Create a policy for various emergency scenarios so you don't respond off-the-cuff or volunteers make things up as they go. You want clear guidelines and expectations for how to respond. When Brian shows up in your office and asks, "Do we know what to do in case of a fire?" you can point to your policies and offer clear answers.
- *Practice.* A written policy helps because it forces you to think through the steps in advance. But as you know, what's on paper doesn't always translate well in real life. Run a fire evacuation or an active-shooter drill and put your policies to the test. Is what you put on paper helpful, or does it not work? Drills help volunteers learn what to do by walking through the actual steps. Change scenarios around. What if fire blocks one of your entrances or doesn't allow an exit from a classroom?
- *Recruit the congregation's help.* If a child has a violent allergic reaction to peanuts or gets a nasty cut from an accident, is there a doctor or nurse in the building who can help? The medical personnel in the worship service know that when 888 flashes on the sanctuary monitors,

> we have a medical emergency on the children's ministry floors. They rush to the main children's ministry desk to lend a hand. Or if you have two hundred young children on your children's floor, consider setting up a team of fathers and other men who will rush to clear out the infant and young toddler rooms during a fire evacuation.

Let's consider two scary scenarios—a fire and an active shooter. What should you keep in mind?

Example 1: fire safety

Fires are extremely dangerous.[1] Churches are especially vulnerable because church buildings often go unoccupied for much of the week. According to the US Fire Administration, fire strikes 1,300 churches every year, causing $38 million in damages.[2] Fire safety protocols and prevention measures can save lives. So take this seriously. Don't skim this information.

Arson is the leading cause of fires in churches, followed by mechanical failures. Other causes of church fires include old wiring in buildings that can't handle the electrical demands, extension cords, carelessness with candles or holiday decorations, and people covering up crimes like burglary.[3] Older church facilities, built before fire codes required sprinklers and noncombustible construction, are susceptible to quick-spreading flames. If you meet in an older building, it is crucial to think through where a fire could block an escape route and devise an alternate plan.

Consider the following fire safety guidelines to protect the children in your care.

1. Invest in fire safety equipment.

Enhance detection before trouble shows up. Do you have early warning systems (like smoke or carbon monoxide detectors) and fire prevention equipment (like extinguishers and sprinklers) throughout the children's area?[4]

2. *Regularly inspect.*

As you inspect, consider the following elements:[5]

- *Structural*: Make sure doors open outward to allow a quick exit in case of a fire. Check that doorways are clearly marked with "EXIT" signs and unobstructed. In your hallways, put signs with escape routes and floor plans, so it is evident to the childcare volunteers and teachers. Verify that renovations, additions, or remodeling follow fire codes and are inspected by a fire marshal.
- *Housekeeping*: Don't use combustible decorations, especially around the holidays. Don't put flammable items (like cloth or paper decorations, drapes, or rugs) near light sockets, outlets, wiring, or other sources of heat. Check that your upholstery and furnishings are made of a fire-retardant fabric. On the same day (or at least within a few days), clean up the debris and garbage and put it all in the proper receptacles outside of the building. Be sure that kitchen areas are cleaned and maintained in good condition (especially stoves, burners, or ventilation hoods).
- *Electrical*: Don't let the electrical or extension cords get frayed, worn out, or dried out. (If they are then throw them out and replace them!) Verify that all the major appliances (air conditioners, refrigerators, etc.) are properly grounded. Look at extension cords and power strips to make sure they are not overloading your circuits. Make sure all of the wall sockets and light switches are covered with plates. If your building is older than thirty years, get the wiring inspected by a qualified electrician.
- *Fire Prevention*: Inspect early warning systems (like smoke detectors) and test to ensure they are in working order and batteries are charged. Hardwire your safety equipment to a circuit in your building. This will eliminate the need to change batteries regularly. If you do have battery-operated equipment, consider changing the batteries twice a year,

once at the turn of the new year and again on July 4th, or install new batteries when you change the time on your clock to adjust for daylight savings. Ensure extinguishers are in easy-to-reach locations,[6] clearly visible, and the operating instructions are close by and legible. Inspect your extinguishers regularly and take notes on the inspections. At least yearly, have a professional also inspect, test, and recharge extinguishers, and put notes on the tag attached to the extinguishers.

3. Run a fire safety drill.

Think through the fire safety routes and come up with a plan. Then execute a drill, which familiarizes volunteers with exit routes and how to react properly.

4. Do a fire safety meeting once a year.

Gather your key staff and leaders annually to talk through evacuation plans and examine fire safety equipment (e.g., inspect early warning systems, identify the location of extinguishers, and look for fire hazardous material, like frayed extension cords, etc.).

5. Write a fire safety policy.

Get a fire professional (like fire marshal) to look it over, and then stick to your policy standards. If you say you'll do a fire drill once a year, then do it.

6. Talk to firemen and your property insurance company.

See if these professionals will do a risk assessment, walk through your building with you to offer tips, and help you think about how best to prevent fires.

Let's make this practical: plan a great escape[7]

Because it's so unusual for children's ministry to practice a fire drill, we've included specifics of how to set up this practice. Use this as a starting checklist to help you prepare and conduct a drill.

We'd encourage you to run the drill during the worship service. This allows you to come as close as possible to imitating a real-life situation that requires evacuation. When you first introduce this idea to your senior pastor, patiently and lovingly persuade him of the value of preparing in advance.

Things to consider before a fire drill (or a real fire):

- Think through the building plan and the best routes to evacuate the building, as well as the designated meeting areas outside of the building for the different age groups. Write this into your evacuation plan.
- Put up proper signage in the children's ministry classrooms and hallways. The signs should describe what to do and what routes to take during a fire.
- Assign responsibilities so everyone knows their role during an actual fire. For example, who will call emergency services? Who will escort the children to designated safety zones? Who will organize the evacuation team as they arrive to help out the childcare workers?
- Plan for the possibility of inclement weather during a real fire. Don't assume a good weather plan will always work.
- Make sure whatever plan you develop works in sync with the other operative emergency plans, like the adults evacuating the sanctuary during a fire.
- Do you have the proper fire evacuation equipment? You can purchase wagons or baby carriers to carry multiple infants out at one time, cribs on wheels, or walking ropes with handles for young children to hold on to as they evacuate the building.
- Train your key leaders, volunteers, and evacuation teams (if you have them). Make sure they all know what to do.
- On your annual fire safety day, do a walkthrough of the drill. Get your children's ministry team to outfit the equipment and walk the routes. If you are using technology, make sure it works.

- As mentioned previously, write your best practices into a fire evacuation policy. Make sure someone in your church's leadership reads your policy and signs off on it.
- Designate a rally point that is far enough away from danger. For a fire emergency, this could be in your parking lot.
- Notify parents of your fire drill plan ahead of time. On the day of the drill, tell the congregation at the start of the service, so no one is surprised when they hear the pitter-patter of little feet in and out of the building.

What to do during a drill:

- Conduct a drill during your busiest times to see if your plan holds up before the real thing happens.[8] But pick a time that's least disruptive for the preaching. Run the drill prior to your pastor's sermon so there would be no distraction for the adults in hearing God's Word preached.
- Just a few minutes before the drill, have a team leader walk through and notify each volunteer with a few basic instructions. Yes, that's right—we're going to catch the workers by surprise. This gets them operating closer to a real-life scenario. You may even hold a second unannounced drill the week after to see how your ministry responds without any warning at all.
- Make sure the volunteers do a headcount of the children *before* walking out of the building.
- Don't run the drill during inclement weather. We do a drill only during the warmer months, when the temperature is optimal for the children being outside.
- Do a second headcount *after* the volunteers and children have arrived at the designated safe meeting areas.
- After the headcount is complete, if everyone is accounted for, the leader in charge gives the "all clear" signal for everyone to return to the building.

What to do after the drill:

- Evaluate how the process went so you are prepared for the real thing. Be humble enough to admit where you can improve.
- Rewrite the fire safety policy to reflect any changes that need to be made.

A few additional items during a real evacuation:

- You'll want to communicate with the parents in the sanctuary so there is no confusion. You might have the service leader say: "The children's wing is being evacuated (give reason). Do not get your children now, or you will slow down the evacuation. In a few minutes, we will give you the all-clear to meet your children, and we will tell you where to meet them (either back in their classrooms or their designated safety zones)."
- You'll want a system (group texting or a digital display monitor in the sanctuary that displays a fire evacuation number, like 999) that notifies all of the appropriate parties who need to be involved.

Example 2: active shooter

According to the Gun Violence Archive (GVA),[9] there were over six hundred mass shootings in the US in 2020. GVA's criteria for a mass shooting requires that at least four people are shot, not including the shooter. Mass shootings occur in businesses, government offices, at public events, and yes, in churches. Preparing your workers to respond to an active shooter incident will save lives.

An evacuation plan only works when the shooter is far away from the children's evacuation path. If there is an active shooter, evacuating children from their classrooms could be potentially dangerous. We might mistakenly send kids directly into the line of fire. At the same time, traditional lockdown methods of shelter in place can leave children vulnerable to an approaching shooter when they could have safely evacuated through a back door.

Each incident is different. Equip your workers to be ready for various possibilities. This can save lives. The Department of Homeland Security promotes a "Run, Hide, Fight"[10] strategy where the victim's response varies depending on the situation. The Federal Emergency Management Agency (FEMA) offers a free course on responding to an active shooter that you can take online.[11]

Consider the following five guidelines in preparing for an active shooter.

1. Get trained on how to respond to an active shooter.

Take the FEMA course and require your staff to take the course as well. Seek out the help of ALICE[12] to train your church on how to respond. For example, never assume the loud "Bang, Bang, Bang," you hear coming from the church foyer is "fireworks." When was the last time you ever heard of a person setting off fireworks in a church lobby?

2. Modify your fire evacuation plan.

In addition to posting fire evacuation routes in classrooms and hallways, add active shooter emergency evacuation routes that include first-floor windows that open or break to provide a way of escape should the fire evacuation path lead you into danger.

3. Outfit your classroom and be prepared.

Installing emergency window shades on classroom doors can prevent a shooter from sizing up a room. Be prepared to move furniture closer to the door to block a doorway in a short amount of time. Post the classroom number inside the class and on the exterior windows to help your teachers identify their room number in an emergency. These postings can provide rescue personnel the information they need to locate your classroom from the building's exterior.

4. Draft an active shooter response policy.

A fire evacuation plan is not sufficient to carry over to an active-shooter event. Bottom line: you need a separate plan. Require your workers to read your new plan and alert your church to the policy's core principles. For example, it is standard procedure to evacuate during a fire, but evacuation may or may not be the best response in an active shooter situation. In a fire evacuation you use the doors and hallways, but in an active shooter situation, you may need to exit through first-floor windows if the danger is coming from the normal fire exit.

5. Work with local law enforcement.

Contact your local police department. Offer them a copy of your building's floor plan marked with accurate room numbers and the children's location. Ensure all of your members know they should call 911 in the event of an emergency.

Don't allow all you have on your plate to prevent you from taking the first step to take the hour-long FEMA training course, contacting law enforcement, and writing out a policy. A little bit of work and training can go a long way in preparing you for an actual shooter on the premises.

What other emergencies might I face?

The room starts shaking so violently things fall off the walls, children fall to the floor, and people start screaming. An earthquake.

Sirens go off in your community and you run to take cover in a basement. A tornado.

An explosion rips through the lobby and you can hear people screaming. A bomb.

A child suddenly falls over, and his head and arms start shaking violently. A seizure.

Add to this a fire or an active shooter, and you may become overwhelmed. The sad reality is that any of these scenarios might happen under your roof. Do everything you can to steward the children entrusted to your care, knowing it may not be possible to foresee every contingency. At the end of the day, our greatest hope needs to be in the care and protection of the Lord over our children.

Give Thought to Your Steps

"All clear." I (Deepak) looked up and down the street. Children were standing in several fenced-in front yards, with thoughtful volunteers monitoring each group of kids. With guidance from our team leaders, the childcare workers and children migrated back into the church building.

I stood there with a satisfied feeling. We'd just run our first live fire drill. That's a big deal. I had been caught flat-footed by Brian early that year, when he had asked if we were ready to respond in the case of a fire. The answer that day had been no. Today it was yes.

As I walked into the church to debrief with our team leaders, Solomon's proverb was on my mind: "The simple believes everything, but the prudent gives thought to his steps" (Proverbs 14:15 NIV).

The simple man may think, *This is so rare—why bother running a drill?* or *I've got so many other things to deal with—I don't have time!* I don't want to be foolish when it comes to being prepared for emergencies. Do you?

Wisdom says, "Because disasters do happen, we're going to get prepared," and "Safety is our number one goal, so we'll be ready when it hits." Wisdom won't give in to laziness, busyness, poor planning, or outright ignorance. Instead, wisdom thinks. It reads. It talks. It plans. It prepares. It prays. And finally, it acts.

But this is more than just being responsible. We're accountable to God, the Judge of the entire universe. He cares about what we do in our children's ministry, because the Lord loves our children even more than we do. In the shadow of the cross, personal responsibility gives way to faithfulness. Because God is faithful and committed, so are we. We'll do everything we can to be counted as faithful on the final day.

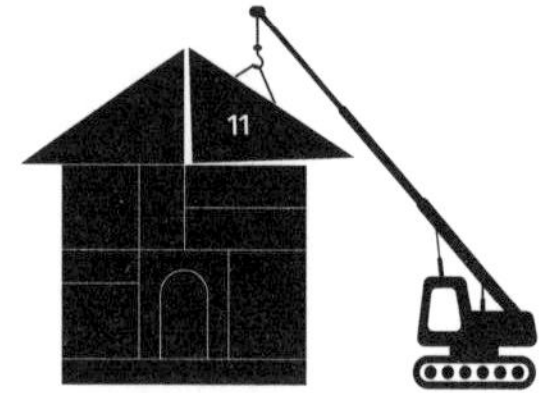

11. Manage the Classroom

Greg walked up to the classroom to pick up his daughters, Emmie and Georgia. He ducked when a paper plane flew by his head. As he looked in, the teacher pleaded with Tommie, who stood on a table, and Carl, who crumbled up paper and threw it at other students. Two other boys, Lawrence and Judson, ran through the room, one chasing the other in a game of tag.

"Oh, my." Greg's anxious eyes moved around the room to find his daughters. He mumbled under his breath, "This place is a zoo." Fortunately, no one in the noisy room heard him. He ushered Emmie and Georgia out the door as quick as possible.

Among the many things necessary for children's ministry, running an orderly, thoughtful, and fun classroom is close to the top of the priority list. Kids don't naturally follow the rules or act respectfully. Their sin messes up the luxurious possibility of a well-ordered and well-behaved classroom.

Sunday school volunteers are earnest Christians with no professional training on how to run a classroom of children. If you supervise two kids, that's not a big deal. If you've got a classroom of fifteen, however, then there's much more to manage. You can't spout off a few directions, read a few verses, and hover

over the kids for fifty minutes. That won't do. The kids need thoughtful guidance and classroom leadership.

This chapter is a concise overview of classroom management.[1] The children's ministry director must train teachers in how to handle behavioral challenges in the classroom. Behavioral problems are roadblocks to a good experience in children's ministry. So we'll think carefully about how to develop a healthy classroom environment and effectively manage behavior.

Our ultimate goal is not orderliness and good behavior. Order, routine, and structure are a means to a much greater end—we desire a well-run classroom *so that we can teach and model the gospel*. Classroom discipline won't change our student's fallen hearts. But the gospel message presented in a well-ordered classroom can do just that.

Establishing a Healthy Classroom Environment

What creates a good classroom experience? What makes things run smoothly? What facilitates gospel-learning and removes the normal distractions of fidgety children?

A well-run classroom requires five components—love, leadership, expectations, routine, and fun.

Begin with love

Communicate your affection for the children in your classroom and ensure your teachers and helpers know to do the same. We heard a wise teacher once say, "You get more of what you encourage." Shouting orders and threats at the kids may command their improved behavior, but it won't win their hearts. To borrow Paul's analogy—if I have all classroom order and command all strict obedience "but have not love, I am a noisy gong or a clanging cymbal" (1 Corinthians 13:1).

Paul regularly expressed his affection for the believers under his care. He spoke of the saints tenderly, as his own children: "We were gentle among you, like a nursing mother taking care of her own children" (1 Thessalonians 2:7). If Paul spoke this way to the adults, how much more should we relate to the children in our classrooms with encouragement and affection?

Exercise leadership

Adults are responsible for what goes on in the classroom, not the kids. God demonstrates good and loving authority toward us, and then calls us to do the same. The Lord entrusts adults with children's lives and charges these adults with their kids' discipline and training for their good. This requires leadership. If an adult is not willing to lead the children, then he or she shouldn't volunteer. We've said to our Sunday school teachers, "You're the boss, so act like it."

There is a temptation for any adult to goof around, act like a kid, and be silly. While there is certainly a time to laugh and have fun with the kids, if you don't act like an adult, you won't be respected by the children. Thus, adults should act like adults. They should take charge because God has given them a benevolent authority to lead and love little children.

Offer clear expectations

Teachers need to set out a few basic classroom expectations for their children. Some expectations are explicit: We listen during story time. We listen to the teacher and other kids. Don't talk over others. Raise your hands if you have a question. We share with one another. We will treat everyone—adults and kids alike—with respect. Some expectations are more implicit: You should do what is asked of you. You can't ignore the teachers.

Make your expectations clear and review them together at the start of every meeting. In some classrooms, we've seen the expectations in big, bold letters on a large posterboard mounted to the wall. That makes it easy for everyone to know what's being asked of them, giving the children a visual cue when the posterboard says in large font:

RESPECT EVERYONE
LISTEN AND BE PATIENT
SHARE AND BE KIND
RAISE YOUR HANDS WHEN YOU HAVE A QUESTION

Expectations are only useful if you review them and reinforce them. Peter reviewed expectations at the start of his first-grade Sunday school class. About fifteen minutes later, as he taught on Jesus's death on the cross, all ten kids listened and paid attention. He paused and affirmed the kids for their outstanding behavior. "I really appreciate how you are sitting so quietly and listening to our lesson!" Kids thrive on encouragement and positive reinforcement.

When adults are inconsistent about their expectations, they not only hurt their students; they hurt themselves as well. Some adults are lenient because they don't want to be viewed as strict, mean, and miserly. Yet, no surprise—if an adult sets low expectations and is inconsistent, the kids will follow suit. This same adult will get run over by the kids, who take advantage of a loose and carefree environment.[2]

Kids need consistency. It's crucial for a teacher to stick to his or her expectations. For older children, the teacher can come up with the expectations with her students, which gives the children greater ownership of their mutually created expectations.[3]

Low expectations, excessive leniency, and inconsistency can ruin a classroom. A teacher shouldn't be intimidated by high expectations, so long as they are undergirded by positive reinforcement, consistency, grace, and love.

When children refuse to abide by classroom expectations, involve their parents. As teachers, we carry a small measure of delegated authority, but we should leave a students' discipline to their parents. Don't hesitate to call in parents from a service or speak to them when they arrive to pick up their child. Here are a few pointers to use when engaging parents:

- Assume the best of a parent and that they want a report on their child's classroom behavior. You can say, "I knew you would want to be informed when Logan had a hard time following our classroom expectations."
- Outline the child's behavior but don't assign a motive, label, or judge the child. Say, "When I asked Logan to share with the other children, he answered, 'No, they don't share with me,' and then he refused to participate and join the reading circle. That is when I thought it best to ask you to speak with him."
- Encourage the parent. You can thank them for their care toward their child, make a comment regarding the difficulties you faced in parenting your own children, and assure them of God's love for them and their children and how much we need the Spirit of God to help us.
- Ask the parent to sit in the class. On a few occasions, we've asked the parents to join the class to help mentor the child through the class, and to also help the teacher understand how best to shepherd and care for this specific child. There is a lot the teacher can pick up by observing a parent discipling his or her child.

Establish a classroom routine

Consider two scenarios. In the first scenario, Little Johnny walks into a classroom, and the teacher says, "Just do whatever you want for now." Johnny—who is normally a nervous child—wonders, *What should I do now? What are the other kids doing?* You sense his anxiety rising as he faces the uncertainty of the moment.

In the second scenario, Little Johnny has attended his first-grade classroom for six months. He knows their initial activity—they always work on a coloring-page for the first five minutes of class. Once enough students have come, the teacher, Mr. Jones, begins with "Good morning class," and he then reminds the children about the classroom expectations. This well-established routine has been the start of every class for the last six months. Johnny knows what to do (color) and when to do it (as soon as he walks in) and for how long to do it (until Mr. Jones says, "Good morning class"). He knows the routine, so there's no uncertainty when he arrives.

Children thrive with order, structure, and predictability, like in the second scenario. It helps them to succeed. A free-for-all (like in the first scenario) is not good for kids. This leads to chaos, anxiety, and frustration for adults and children alike. If Johnny knows the what, when, and why of his first-grade Sunday school class, it provides him with a sense of security and protects him from the anxiety of the unknown. A well-established structure and routine make the class predictable for Johnny, and therefore safer and more enjoyable.[4]

It might be helpful to put the schedule in big, bold letters on a posterboard on the classroom wall so that it's visible to all. That will be useful for new teachers, like Mr. Jones. In his first few weeks of teaching, he would pause and look over at the schedule to remind himself what the class should be doing next. Because the posterboard sported big and bold letters, Mr. Jones could see it from any spot in the classroom.

Welcome Time –	*Sit quietly*
Worship Time –	*Sing enthusiastically*
Story Time –	*Listen carefully*
Craft Time –	*Work diligently*
Snack Time –	*Eat Politely*
Review Time –	*Think carefully*
Free Time –	*Whisper quietly*
Pick up Time –	*Wait patiently*

Keep your lessons engaging and fun

Suppose Mr. Jones, in a humdrum, monotone voice read the David and Goliath story (1 Samuel 17) to ten first-grade children for thirty-six minutes. What would happen? Even though it is an exciting story, the kids would get fidgety and distracted in a matter of minutes. A few kids might start making faces at each other or start poking each other. They'd get restless and frustrated the longer Mr. Jones's voice droned on.

Teachers must proactively think about how to make the classroom experience engaging. For example, in a typical first-grade classroom, you'll get a mixture of kids who can read and those who can't. What if Mr. Jones stood on a chair for all of Goliath's lines and growled as he spoke them? How would the children react? Their eyes would be laser-focused on his presentation.

It's also okay to give the children who can't read a piece of paper to draw on while you present the lesson. Mr. Jones could say, "For those of you who can't read, draw this story while I read it aloud. For those of you who can read, open your Bible and follow along." The drawing helps the nonreaders, since they can't make sense yet of words on a page. That way everyone is engaged in the text at some level.[5]

Kids love to see, touch, move, wiggle, draw, cut, glue, paint, and color. Here are a few other ways Mr. Jones could make learning more fun and engaging:

- Have the children act out Goliath's defiant cries ("I defy the ranks of Israel this day!") and David's slinging of a stone at Goliath's head.
- Pass around props like Saul's armor to try on or David's sling and a stone to touch and feel.
- Introduce a snack that represents different parts of a story—like a gummy bear, who is David (the tiny guy who is tough!), and a banana, who is Goliath (bigger and stronger).

God is the point of the story, not these different creative methods, yet creativity makes learning more enjoyable. If the teacher makes the lesson fun, the kids are less likely to misbehave and more likely to stay engaged. It creates a better overall classroom experience for everyone.

Practical Strategies to Effectively Manage Classroom Behavior

If you witness a master teacher at work, you'll note they are excellent at their trade, not just because of what they say but also how they manage their students' behavior. What strategies should we employ to slow down misbehavior and keep things moving along?

Deploy helpers

Make sure the helpers assigned to a classroom actively engage the children as Mr. Jones teaches. Let's say a child, Tommy, spins in his chair. What can a helper do to refocus the child so that Mr. Jones doesn't have to stop teaching? Sally, the helper, can walk over and whisper instructions like, "Look at Mr. Jones" and "Stay in your chair." With a smile on her face, she can gently tap Tommy on the shoulder and gesture for him to look forward at Mr. Jones.

Remind helpers to move around as needed. Sally can walk through the class while Mr. Jones teaches. Parents and teen volunteers will often stand in the back of the classroom where the children can't see them. Or, if Mr. Jones teaches younger children and the kids are all sitting around Mr. Jones, like at story time, have your helper Sally sit among the children, too.

Give your helpers cues to help distracted children. Imagine little Sam kicks the chair of the child in front of him. Mr. Jones calls out to Mary (one of the parent helpers), "Could you help Sam with his chair?" Mary can address Sam privately, so that Mr. Jones can continue with the lesson.

Position yourself so you can scan the entire class

Kids get away with things when the teacher is not paying attention or not looking at the class. Mr. Jones buries his face in his Bible as he reads and often looks down at his teaching notes for a long time. Every time he looks down, he gives a child the opportunity for misbehavior.

What's the alternative? The teacher can position himself so he can make eye contact with every set of eyes in the room. Teaching expert Doug Lemov calls this a teacher's "radar." The teacher makes a habit to pause and scan the class, looking across the classroom to see what every student is doing.[6]

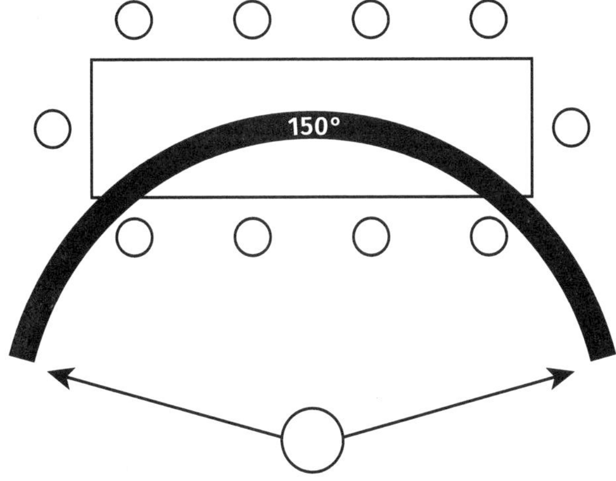

You've heard the adage, "A teacher has eyes in the back of his head!" If you know your anatomy, you know that's not possible (except in *Star Wars*). Instead, what's happening is the teacher employs his radar. He engages with everyone in the room and consistently scans the class.[7]

Actively employ nonverbal signals to head off bad behavior

A good teacher uses noninvasive management to head off misbehavior—eye contact, a slight nod of the head, or a hand motion.[8] First-grader Tommy turns and punches his classmate Carl on his shoulder. The punch hurts, and it's meant to provoke a reaction. At that moment, Mr. Jones has a choice to let Tommy's infraction go or do something about it. We've all been in a class when the drama of one child's misbehavior distracts from the teaching. Mr. Jones could call out Tommy's name, but that draws the whole class's attention and breaks his flow of teaching.

Because this is typical behavior for Tommy, Mr. Jones points at Tommy with his right hand, narrows his eyes, and raises his eyebrows while he looks directly at Tommy. His goal is to employ nonverbal communication to correct Tommy's behavior and keep the class moving along. That means no break in his teaching. He juggles both correction and instruction simultaneously, which makes the interaction with Tommy much less disruptive to the rest of the class.

Articulate directions that are concrete and visible[9]

A thoughtful teacher offers directions that are tangible and specific, not anything vague. Ambiguity allows a student to ignore a teacher's instructions or corrections. The teacher also articulates things in a way that makes the student's compliance visible. It's helpful to say, "Bibles open in front of you," rather than, "Bibles out." Likewise, say something like, "I want to see your crayons moving," instead of, "You should be drawing."[10]

When the teacher offers multistep directions, he prefaces it with something like, "When I say 'go,' I want you to X, Y, and Z. Now go!" Otherwise, the students will get started on X and miss Y and Z, and it gets a little crazy.[11]

Correct with the most subtle, least noticeable, and least invasive means possible[12]

A good teacher minimizes classroom drama. As much as possible, correction should be invisible, and teaching and classroom activities continue uninterrupted. The more the teacher keeps things moving in the class, the better. Consider the following means of correction, from least to most invasive.

Nonverbal intervention. We offered this example earlier, when Mr. Jones moved next to Tommy and used a hand gesture and a stern glance to get Tommy back on track, without any break in his teaching.[13] Sometimes you can stop a kid from doing what he or she shouldn't be doing by simply walking over and standing by them. The correction comes from this teacher's presence next to the child.[14]

A short, positive class redirection. By "short," we mean there's an economy of language—a statement that's brief, concise, and to the point. And the directions are not aimed at one student but addresses the entire class. Let's say Tommy and Carl are goofing off. Rather than singling them out, Mr. Jones can say, "Everyone should be coloring," or "Eye contact with me please," or "Please sit upright." This is much better than picking on one overactive student, drawing all of the class's attention, and distracting from the lesson.[15]

Anonymous group correction. This again is correction without calling out a specific name. Instead, it's anonymous. Mr. Jones comments, "Follow me, please" (a positive class redirection). "I need two more eyes on me" (anonymous group correction). And if the student turns to the teacher, a nonverbal signal, like a head nod or a smile, can help reinforce the student's positive step.[16] Suppose multiple kids are misbehaving at the same time. In that case, you can stop the class and remind the students of the class expectations by saying something like, "Let's stop for a second so that everyone can focus again and remember not to talk when someone else is speaking."[17]

Private individual correction (PIC). Unfortunately, if an individual correction is necessary, the teacher will have to stop his or her teaching if another adult helper is not available. (Remember, the goal is to keep things going.) Let's say the feud between first-graders Tommy and Carl continues—Carl seeks revenge for Tommy's punch by flicking erasers at Tommy. Mr. Jones gets the class to work independently or in small groups. He then comes alongside Carl to address the problem. Mr. Jones (who stands almost six feet tall) crouches down and uses a soft tone to correct Carl. "Let's stop throwing erasers and let me see your pen moving." A short, concrete, and visible instruction will often get the job done. By bending down, Mr. Jones gets on Carl's level rather than hovering over him. And the gentle tone or whisper makes the conversation more private.[18]

Lightning-quick public correction. If a teacher must correct a student more publicly, then he does it quickly and focuses the misbehaving student on the positive behavior that he or she should be doing. And for the sake of the rest of the students, whose attention is drawn to this public correction, the teacher also directs everyone's attention to behavior he most wants exemplified by the class. "Jonathan, I need you drawing right now . . . just like I see the rest of the class doing!"[19]

The teacher can't just ignore misbehavior by praising what's good in the classroom. He or she has to deal with bad behavior and catch misconduct as early as possible. Bad behavior is likely to persist, so the teacher deals with it when it's first starting, not letting things snowball.[20]

The teacher always exemplifies a gracious disposition, even during correction. He or she should be firm and calm, not agitated and frustrated.[21]

Add to this gracious disposition a smile and a "please" and "thank you." A smile communicates, "I'm glad to be here, and I've got a plan." A scowl communicates, "I didn't want this assignment," and "I'm expecting you all to misbehave."[22]

Adding "please" and "thank you" shows respect and adds civility to the teacher's instructions. Mr. Jones offers instructions like, "Hands folded in front of you, Maya." And then quietly adds, "Thank you." The "thank you" reinforces the positive behavior and reestablishes what is expected.[23]

Regain control of the class and help them to refocus

Every teacher (even the good ones!) has experienced a rowdy class and felt like he's losing control of his students. At this moment, a teacher's instinct can be to press through, talk over the kids, and force things to move along—but that won't work!

A better option is to slow things down and regain control of the class by *waiting out the students*. First graders Tommy, Carl, and Maya get worked up. Mr. Jones stops his teaching or the coloring activity and says, "I'm going to wait until you're ready." He restates the classroom expectation and waits for obedience. Mr. Jones keeps repeating it until he gets quiet. It's a battle of wills. He waits the kids out, which requires his patience and determination to regain control. After the class becomes silent, Mr. Jones says, "Thank you for giving me your attention. I'm really excited about our lesson today, and I'm glad you are ready to listen." Keep in mind, he does all of this with gracious disposition. There is no need for him to be heavy-handed.[24]

Another way to regain control is to use an *attention getter*, which quickly gains the focus of the students without costing Mr. Jones a ton of energy. Mr. Jones teaches a call and response, like: "1, 2, 3 . . . eyes on me!" And students have been taught to respond: "1, 2 . . . eyes on you!"[25] Or he can say something like, "If you can hear my voice, clap once." (A few kids will clap, which gets the attention of other kids.) Mr. Jones continues, "If you are listening, clap twice." (A few more kids will join in.) Usually by the time Mr. Jones offers three claps (or barks or stomps or donkey noises), he has the attention of the entire class.[26]

Teaching for Life

The classroom strategies taught here won't come naturally to your volunteer teachers. You'll need to encourage, train, and reinforce these skills. Yet, if you help them, and consistently reinforce these things, you will reap helpful benefits in due time. While teaching is a gift to some folks, just about any volunteer can hold the children's attention if he or she adds a bit of creativity and deploys the strategies we've presented in this chapter.

Set a goal to equip and strengthen your teachers and class helpers. Provide feedback when you can. Visit their classrooms and watch your teachers present their lessons. That will provide an opportunity to offer them suggestions for improving their presentation and classroom management. When you get an experienced teacher who effectively engages the children, assign your less experienced teachers as helpers in their classroom to watch and learn.

We want to remove obstacles to Bible teaching and presentation of gospel truths. Learning these effective classroom strategies is just a start. Remember, our ultimate goal is not order or good behavior but facilitating an opportunity for children to hear and know God.

Now let's go back to Greg, from the opening illustration of this chapter. This time Greg waits at the classroom door to pick up his daughters Emmie and Georgia for an early exit. He sees Mr. Jones standing on a chair, shouting Goliath's charge from 1 Samuel 17:10 with a gravelly voice. The children are engaged and laughing. His daughters don't even notice that Greg is there.

Instead of whisking his girls out for their trip to their uncle's wedding, he waits to allow Mr. Jones to finish this teaching segment. Greg notices the classroom's helpers moving around to keep distracted children engaged, the kids raising hands rather than shouting out, and Mr. Jones communicating the gospel effectively. Greg stays just outside the classroom door, and he thinks, *What a great experience for my girls!*

BONUS TEACHER HELPS

Pop Quiz: What would your teachers do in these problematic situations?

Use the following list of common problems to talk through with your teachers what they would do in each scenario and what expectations they might set up. These hypothetical situations can help your volunteers better anticipate the challenges that are likely to come their way.

- *Separation anxiety*. A sweet two-year-old, Alina, stands just outside the classroom. She's nervous and not wanting to go into the room.
- *Physical harm*. Donovan hits or bites another child.
- *Conflict*. Four-year-olds Pete and Steven are pulling at the same toy and arguing with each other. Pete screams, "I want this car!" Steven attempts to yank it out of his tight grip, yelling, "No, I want it!"
- *Rowdiness*. The students are not listening or raising hands, and the kids are talking out of turn in group discussions.
- *Everyone "needs" to go the bathroom*. Pete asks to go the restroom. Almost immediately, two other kids say they "need" to go also. Is it really wise to send three boys all together at the same time?
- *Inconsolable child*. Little Suzy is crying for her mother, no matter how you try to comfort her. Even worse, another kid or two also starts to cry because of Suzy.

BONUS TEACHER HELPS

Additional Tips on Becoming a Better Teacher

- *Pray.* Praying may seem like a perfunctory step to some, but we want to do more than fill children's minds with a good lesson. We want to transform their lives. That's the part only God can do. We're in a partnership with God each time we enter the classroom. It's best to ask for his help every time we teach.
- *Prepare.* We'll have some days when we grab our lesson, run into class, and read it from the page. But that should be the rare exception. Be familiar enough with your lesson that you're never chained to the pages and can look up and maintain eye contact with the kids. If you haven't read the lesson, prepared the crafts, and thought through the activities, it won't go well. Think ahead and work through the logistics. Read over the materials and ask the other teachers questions. Set up the classroom. Cut, fold, tape, or glue any activities beforehand. Be sure that you're ready before the kids arrive.
- *Know your students.* The younger the kids, the shorter their attention span. So keep it short, simple, and engaging for the younger children. Be aware of incompatible relationships. If Billy and Jared don't do well sitting together, separate them from the start of class. If you have a special needs child, ask the parents for tips to best care for their son or daughter.
- *Engage the students.* It helps if you are energetic, use hand motions, vary your tone and pitch, and move around (rather than quiet, stiff, reserved, and monotone).
- *Stay gospel-focused.* As you descend into practical and tactical teaching (managing a room of kids, teaching content, and so on), don't lose sight of our ultimate goal—to teach

children to know God as Creator, to understand their sin, to see their need for a Savior, and to love Christ. Always keep the gospel in view.

- *Speak to the heart.* We spent time on behavior management in this last chapter. Outward conformity—a child's obedience—is not the same thing as heart transformation. A child is much more than his or her outward behavior. The Bible makes our heart the center of our life. So as you present your lesson, speak to their hearts rather than listing a set of rules to follow. Jesus said it's out of the overflow of the heart that we speak (Matthew 12:34–35; Luke 6:43–45). Out of your heart you think, feel, speak, choose, and do. When you teach and mentor kids, keep the heart as your target.
- *Be a thoughtful reader.* When you read a Bible story, don't rush through the text. Read it at a slow but deliberate pace and emphasize important words. Change your voice to help the children know when various characters of a story are speaking. Even a slight inflection change will make a story come to life.
- *Take leadership.* Be clear, concrete, and direct with instructions. Like a tour guide on a trip, offer guidance throughout the entire class. If they are coloring and need to shift to Bible reading, give them a two-minute warning. Two minutes later, have the kids put the crayons away in bins. Bins go in the middle of the table. Direct them to "zip their lips" and sit on their hands or fold them in front. This is especially necessary with younger children.[27]
- *Plan for contingencies.* It is a good idea to come to class with extra material just in case the worship service goes long, or a helper forgets to bring the craft, or you finish your lesson and activities early. What will you do if you need to fill in time at the end of the class? Have a list of possible fillers ready. Perhaps prepare a generic backup segment or game that you can use for any lesson.

12. Pursue Creative Excellence

"What are you doing here?" I (Marty) asked Mary as she passed through our check-in station. "I thought you were scheduled for surgery this week," I added.

"I did have surgery," she replied. "Everything went fine. I feel great. I'm just a bit tired. I know I told you that I would stay home today, but Jack wouldn't let me. He wanted to come to Promise Kingdom," she said, pointing at our ministry's name on the sign overhead. I looked up at the letters carved into an imitation rock face that forms our two-story children's ministry entrance.

"Besides, it's drama week," Mary further explained. "Jack absolutely loves the Backstage Players. He insisted we come. He wouldn't miss it for the world."

A wave of gratitude to God flooded my heart for all he had enabled us to accomplish and how our efforts were bearing fruit in eager children like Jack. I welcomed Mary back, grateful her outpatient surgery went well. I reflected for a moment on the many years it took our team to put together our program. After spending years focusing on our curriculum, we began thinking of ways to make our space fun and inviting. Each spring, our leaders met to look for one or two elements we could improve. Year by year, we purposed to take another step forward. Folks visiting our ministry today don't realize that what they are experiencing is the product of twenty years of slow but steady progress and improvements.

Things were not always so polished for us. Back in our early church planting days, our ministry didn't have a name, nor did we have a drama team. We spent all our energy loading and unloading plastic crates of supplies to and from each classroom every Sunday. Back then, we held church in an old middle school repurposed as a community center and borrowed space from an adult day-care program. Our classrooms weren't decorated or equipped for kids. As a result, every week we pushed back the adult-sized furniture, hauled in carpets, set up small homemade tables, and delivered bins of supplies. We doused the daycare center's bathrooms with pine cleaner to cover the smell and cleaned up the half-dead roaches that had succumbed to the exterminator's treatments.

In those early days, we did our best to accomplish three main goals (in order of priority): First, provide a safe, well-administrated space for the children. Second, present the gospel through the week's Bible lesson every Sunday. Third, add something creative that will make church a fun place for the kids. The extras, like adding a drama team or worship team, would have to wait. We just didn't have the time or bandwidth.

Although we made a lot of mistakes along the way, we got our priorities right. We focused on those same three primary goals for the first year in our new building before adding the extras we now enjoy. While families visiting for the first time may be initially impressed with our custom-designed entrance, large murals, and drama program, we hope it is the gospel-centered content of our lessons and the excellence of our administration that matters most.

There is a reason we've placed this chapter last in the book. While there is no denying the effect a creative and fun environment can have on kids, it is far more critical to ensure your space is safe and the message the children receive is gospel-rich. You can skip the murals and the drama, but you can't afford to get the gospel content wrong, nor can you afford to shortchange safety.

Keep First Things First

The most important components of what you do weekly are keeping your children safe and secure and presenting a biblical, gospel-rich message. That doesn't mean you can't add a fresh coat of paint, brighten up tired walls, or deploy an eager artist to paint a mural on your children's ministry entrance. But before you focus your energy on flashy decor, make sure the priorities of *safety* and *substance* are covered.

I (Marty) once visited a church that looked like the kids were entering a major theme park. They used professional actors in their drama performances, and their main auditorium looked like a gameshow sound stage. It was clear they gave a lot of attention to their program and presentation. Sadly, their curriculum focused on good morals disconnected from the gospel. They taught the kids to be courageous and kind and honest and trustworthy. While these are important values, taught apart from gospel truths like sin, repentance, faith, and holiness, they form an alternate gospel. The goal is to present biblical truth in a fun and engaging way without compromising content.

Once you have a solid gospel-based curriculum and your child protection policies are firmly established, there is no denying the added impact that a fun and creatively designed environment and program can have on the kids. Fun and creativity keep the children wanting to come back for more—more excitement, more fun, and, yes, more gospel truth.

Choose a Name (and Identity)

Back in the community center, moving those bins around consumed our time. We focused our energy on setting up the classrooms for the teachers before the kids arrived. That meant coming to the building by 7:30 a.m. for our 10 a.m. service. The sound crew got there even earlier. They needed to move their sound equipment carts out of our storage room before we could access the children's ministry bins stacked up against the far wall.

The generic name "Children's Ministry" aptly described our ever-changing mishmash of rooms sprinkled over the former middle school layout of hallways. By God's grace, we never lost a child and survived the long summers without air conditioning. With our move into our new facility, however, it was time to choose a more specific name for our ministry. Most church ministries like the ushers, greeters, or parking lot ministries do well without a special name. Other programs like children's ministry and youth ministries benefit from an identity. A name communicates identity, order, excitement, and can even help you pass along essential values.

Some churches name their ministry to children after the church. A church named Grace Redemption Church might call their ministry to children "Grace Kids." Naming your ministry after your church communicates a oneness of vision and mission. Other churches adopt a mission-oriented name that aligns with the purpose of the ministry. We chose to call our ministry "Promise Kingdom." The word *promise* is a reference back to God's gospel promise first delivered to Adam and Eve, later delivered to Abraham and his offspring, and affirmed by the prophets who foretold of Christ's coming.

The word "kingdom" in our name has a double meaning. A kingdom is a place or location. Therefore "Promise Kingdom" is where God's promises are celebrated and modeled by the teachers who pass them on to the next generation. But the word "kingdom" also refers to the sphere of God's rule and reign. We desire that the gospel we share with the children each Sunday be used by God to expand the kingdom of God into their hearts.

And, for fun, the word "kingdom" lent itself to a safari theme. We purchased loose-fitting button-down khaki shirts with our name embroidered above the right shirt pocket for our coordinators. The uniforms helped us showcase our new name and served to identify our children's ministry director and coordinators to our guests.

Decorate Your Space

While the architect who designed our children's ministry space added colorful floor tiles, the neutral paint on the classroom walls looked bland and uninviting. After focusing for a few years on getting our curriculum set, we began to talk about creating a fun, inviting space whose aesthetic matched the depth of our curriculum theology.

Even though the children's ministry entrance was visible off to the far right, the small check-in table got lost in the cavernous two-story lobby space. Every new family had to ask where to take their children. In our annual brainstorming session, we discussed adding a sign or banner over our entrance. Someone suggested we go all out and add a three-dimensional façade to the two-story lobby wall above the entrance.

I (Marty) pulled my design skills out of the closet and sketched out a ten-foot-high cliff face wall above which two majestic trees stood. Between the two trees, I drew a lion and a lamb—the two images of Christ from Revelation—and across the face of the rock above the doorway, I sketched in our name, Promise Kingdom.

I still have that early sketch on my desk that I presented to the elders, asking for permission to create a fun entrance to our space. One thing led to another, and a year later, our brainstorming session became a reality, and our ministry looked like the entrance to a theme-park ride. While we spent a ton of money to have a set design crew fabricate and install the fiberglass-coated foam façade, it's been serving us for fifteen years, and we don't have plans to change it.

If you can't afford to pay professionals, use the talents of your church members. Though we blew our budget on our entrance, that didn't stop us from using volunteers to add other elements to the space. One fine art student offered to volunteer for a summer, painting murals throughout our ministry. He pulled together a half dozen artist friends and painted over ten feet of murals that summer. Our only expense was for the paint and a few pizza lunches.

I've visited other churches whose space is entirely decorated by the creative volunteers of their church. I've toured jungles and train stations, all constructed and painted with donated talents and time.

Add the Extras

In addition to the entrance and murals, we added extras to our space. Year by year, we brainstormed and added new elements like a portable stage for our grade-school drama team, a large puppet stage for preschool, a worship team, and a creative Bible-memory program. Other churches I know have added sensory rooms for special needs kids, coffee stations for teachers and helpers, lounges for nursing moms, and more.

By adding a new element every year or two, we grew at a manageable pace. And except for our themed entrance, we used volunteers to do the work. A single mom offered to start our drama team. A retired engineer offered to construct our theater stage with a group of dads. They spent hundreds of hours welding our stage. When not in use, the whole thing folds up and can be rolled into a corner of our large assembly room.

The same group of dads built a large puppet theater for our preschool class. Carved from foam and coated with fiberglass, it matches the rock design of our entrance. Gifted folks who are glad to deploy their talents for the kingdom are ripe for the asking in every congregation. Often finding out who they are and asking them to help are the only steps required to deploy their skills. We discovered that one of our members was a former puppet designer. He taught and demonstrated puppeteering to our teachers. Another dad offered to create a custom database for our ministry that we used for years before moving to our current check-in system. One of our coordinators worked in graphic design and was glad to create the graphics we need for our ministry.

Once we have an idea, we look for a champion volunteer to carry that idea to completion. Our champions jumped in to lead our Bible-memory program, small groups for grade school, and our grade-school musical worship program.

Not all the programs I've mentioned are still in operation today. Our Bible-memory program fizzled out when we lost our champion. We still do Bible memory, but it's not the same. But our drama team, "The Backstage Players," staffed by teen actors, continues on. We've turned over three generations of teen actors. Our grade-school kids dream about serving on the drama team one day. When they graduate out of our program after sixth grade, we recruit them for smaller side rolls.

Excel in Administration

Whatever you add to your ministry, be sure to administrate things well. It is far more important to do less with excellence than to do so much that your program suffers. Folks who go to a five-star restaurant but experience two-star service don't return. First-time guests will often decide whether to return solely by their family's first experience with your children's ministry. Doing less with excellence will make a lasting impression. Better to offer a three-star program with five-star quality than the other way around.

Bring on additional creative elements slowly and look for champion volunteers to help you lead new initiatives—don't try to do everything yourself. Look to make your children's ministry excellent in every way before you look to make it bigger. And don't be afraid to pause a program when you lose a key volunteer. Slow and steady growth won't overtax your workers. Pull together your leaders, brainstorm new ideas, pray for a champion to help you, and think of who that might be. Once you come up with names, don't be afraid to approach these individuals with your vision and an invitation to jump in. If God is in it, they'll get excited and take over with joy.

Improving your ministry a bit at a time will bring excellence into your program in a manageable way, spreading the workload around. Your teachers and helpers will serve with joy, and the first-time visitors and their children will leave amazed for all you've accomplished and grateful to God for your service to their family.

Creativity Can Make a Difference

"I know you." Jordan smiled at me (Deepak). He was about four feet tall, with clean-cut brown hair and a beautiful grin across his face. "You were the father who hugged his son."

I stood at my post, Bible in hand, at the back door of our sanctuary. I was greeting church members and children as they walked out the door after our Sunday worship service. I'd often say "hello" to Jordan's dad or mom as they headed past me on their way to the cookie and coffee table. Little kids don't usually say much to me because it's intimidating to talk to the pastor.

We had just finished a busy week of Vacation Bible School (VBS). When the chance to do drama for VBS came along, I jumped on the opportunity. It was a practical and fun way for my teenage kids and I to serve together. With bucketloads of enthusiasm, we put on the most biblically accurate (but also action packed and fun) stories that we could pull off. We got dressed up in full costume, put on accents, and offered an exciting rendition of the stories for these kids. And we endeavored to make the gospel extremely clear, no matter what story we told.

Jordan broke the ice that Sunday morning, and I was delighted. He and I talked about the prodigal son's return to his father (Luke 15), and the father's love and mercy for his lost son. It was a brief conversation, but it was a gospel opportunity with a boy who had never spoken to me before. I have no doubt that the creativity we added to our skits made the gospel truths more memorable for the children at VBS. It clearly had an effect on Jordan.

In glory, will our drama presentation about the prodigal son be a watershed moment of salvation for Jordan? Probably not. But is it one seed, planted in the heart of a sweet little boy, and his journey towards knowing Christ? I do hope so.

If safety and substance are your priority, then creativity can be a wonderful means that the Lord uses to impact the little hearts. Glory be to God.

Self-Evaluation: Pursue Creative Excellence

Putting first things first: Do you have safety and substance taken care of in your children's ministry? If not, what do you need to do to secure these things? What one or two new elements can you add this coming year to improve your creativity in children's ministry?

"Folks who go to a five-star restaurant but experience two-star service don't return." Are you offering a five-star children's ministry with two-star service? Or are you doing less with excellence?

Conclusion
Where Do You Go from Here?

After reading twelve chapters, you're likely contemplating changes in your children's ministry. Whether you're just looking to make a few tweaks and adjustments, or you've caught a vision for a wholesale redirection, it is essential to approach changes with wisdom and care.

As we wrap up our discussion, we offer a few suggestions to help you implement those adjustments to your ministry.

Pray

Don't skip this vital step. You can't do what we've described on your own. You need the Lord's help! Ask him to lead you. Run back to our heavenly Father again and again. Ask for wisdom (James 1:5) and plead with him to show kindness and mercy to you and your ministry.

Discuss

Share what you've read with your pastors above you. Does your church's overall leadership (no matter what form it takes) agree on what philosophy should be driving your children's ministry? If not, you can use this book as a starting place to talk over the direction of your children's ministry. Your goal would be to see your church's entire leadership team have buy-in on the philosophy, content, and safety procedures that undergird your children's ministry.

Take your ministry coordinators and key personnel through chapters that spurred your thinking. Maybe offer a copy of our book to committed parents. Ask them to read it and start a conversation to garner their support for adjustments or redirection. Get others involved in rethinking, creating, planning, and organizing your children's ministry.

Prioritize

Rank the items you'd like to work on in order of priority so you make sure to address vital areas. Then tackle one at a time.

Make Changes over Time

A man can only sprint for a few feet, but he can walk for miles. Don't think you should have gotten everything done yesterday. That's a recipe for needless stress. Be patient. Take a long-term view of change—you can make a small tweak in a day, but more extensive adjustments should be implemented slowly over months and even years.

Don't Go It Alone

Once you've got buy-in from your leaders, spread the work around. Delegate areas to capable people. If you are not sure who that might be, ask your leaders and pastors for suggestions. Ask the Lord to raise up volunteers and then start handing off assignments to responsible people.

Olivia's Story

Why do we think, plan, teach, pray, and work so hard in children's ministry? Because we know the Lord can use adults like us to present beautiful truths of Scripture to our children.

Consider Olivia's story, in her own words.

I loved being a part of the fours and fives Sunday School class when I was younger. I remember how much joy the adults showed in teaching the Bible and how well they got along with each other. I have vivid memories of couples standing in front and leading us in songs like "The B-I-B-L-E" and "Jesus Loves Me" with sign language, which I thought was awesome. We had so much fun singing! During the lessons, I remember them constantly pointing us to the Bible for answers and encouraging us to listen to God's Word. I also remember that Jesus and everything he did for us by coming to earth and dying for our sins was a constant theme—in the lessons, in the singing, and in the questions they asked us. We talked about sin, and I came to a realization of my own sinfulness (particularly towards my little brother!). From everything they taught me about Jesus, I had no doubt that the loving, strong, and good Savior, who died on the cross for me, would forgive me and make me his.

So that brings me back to the kitchen table. When my mom and dad shared the gospel with me, I realized that I had already heard it. I later had my share of questions about whether my decision to follow Jesus as a five-year-old was "real." But looking back now, it's clear to me that it was. To this day, I think my gut-level belief that the Bible is completely reliable and adequate for every situation in our lives comes in part from the way that this group of teachers constantly held up God's Word in that class. I also think that my conviction that Jesus is a real, strong, and loving Savior comes in part from what they taught us about him.

I wish I could let my teachers from long ago know what a difference their joyful, faithful, Jesus-exalting service made in my life. But if that doesn't happen on earth, I'm looking forward to giving them a big, long five-year-old's hug in heaven!

This is why we labor so hard. This is why we organize and recruit, why we teach and sing, and why we plan and pray. In his mercy, God will use our words, our actions, and our example. We'll be a living, real-life demonstration that God is real and that the gospel is true. Because of the great love with which he loves us, the Lord will convert some of our children.

Lean on the master builder. On the hard days, remember what Jesus said: "I will build my church" (Matthew 16:18). Have no doubt about it—God will bring children to saving faith. Remember, you're partnering with the Creator of the universe to accomplish a task he's already committed to achieving. Take comfort in that, and move forward knowing that God will fulfill all of his promises in Christ.

Appendix A
A Brief Word to Church Planters

You've ventured out into the amazing world of church planting. Welcome!

You're building a core team. You're figuring out how to prepare public worship services—lining up the venue, music, greeting, parking, and more. You're hoping the local public school or the community center around the corner will let you rent their building. You're evangelizing the neighborhood, hoping to see conversions. You're meeting non-Christians through your daughter's soccer team.

But on top of all of this, you've got to find a way to build a children's ministry. After all, if you don't have anything for the kids—absolutely *nothing*—then you'll have a hard time retaining families. You want something for families and their kids, but what and how much do you start with?

Here are six guidelines for kick-starting a children's ministry.

1. Find Competent Leaders on Your Core Team and Entrust Them to Launch Your Children's Ministry

For church-planting pastors

Don't take this on by yourself. The typical church planter has a bazillion details to manage as he starts a brand-new gospel witness in a city. He's bursting at the seams, trying to find time to do everything. Starting a children's ministry will involve a ton of details—nursery equipment, child safety, curriculum, classroom organization, volunteer recruitment, and more. *Delegation is key to good leadership*. As a new pastor, there are some crucial tasks you need to engage with (e.g., structuring the church budget, planning the public services, writing sermons), but there are many tasks you can hand off to competent help. Children's ministry certainly falls in the latter category.

While any gifted leader with administrative skills can help form a children's ministry, there are advantages to tapping a married couple for this role. Starting and maintaining a children's ministry is arguably the second most labor-intensive church-planting role. It's more than a one-person job. While you are preaching to twenty adults, your children's ministry leaders will be caring for the children and workers that make up the other 40 percent of your church! Having a husband and wife team can help in relating to both men and women serving in the ministry. Remember, it will largely be married couples with their children who will visit your children's ministry. Having another couple greet these guests and talk about family will put visitors at ease.

Look for a couple (or an individual if a couple is not available) who is spiritually mature, administratively gifted, reliable, and competent. Spiritual maturity is vital, but if they are administratively inept, that will hurt everything! If you don't have a couple on your team that fits the job description, consider specifically recruiting a couple gifted in these areas to join your church plant to take on this enormous task.

When you've found people to take this on, ask them for a two-year commitment. A two-year term will make it less likely your newly appointed leaders will resign six months into your church plant. The two-year term also provides an end date for their assignment. If all goes well, they might renew for a second two-year term, and perhaps even longer.

Don't wait till the month before your launch to look for a leader. Make finding your children's ministry leadership one of the first things you do. Identify your leaders six months or even a year before your launch date. This will give them time to train and plan. Encourage them to shadow the children's ministry director from your sending church for a minimum of three months of on-the-job training.

Meet with your new leaders monthly for updates and care. Make sure they are balancing their own spiritual well-being, family needs, and the demands of a new ministry. Don't let them burn out.

Don't let this couple (or individual) attempt to build the children's ministry on their own. Encourage them to recruit a few people from your core team. Their first goal is to develop a children's ministry leadership team—a few competent and servant-hearted souls who want to serve the church plant in this way. Help them pick a few people from the core team and then encourage this start-up team to plan and pray together.

For the children's ministry leaders

Thank you for taking on this responsibility for your pastor. What you need to know from your pastor is what level of involvement he wants in the initial decisions. Here are some possibilities:

- *Option 1:* Your pastor says, "I *completely* delegate this to you." Maybe your church-planting pastor is so overwhelmed by what he's doing he needs you to take full responsibility for everything in children's ministry. As you saw in our chapter about pastoral leadership (ch. 4), we don't encourage pastors to fully disengage from children's ministry. It's vital to have *some* pastoral oversight. Press for meetings to give your pastor updates and ask critical questions. Plan them out a month or two ahead of time to make it easier to fit them in his schedule.

- *Option 2:* Your pastor says, "I'll be involved on a macro level." He sets the course for where things need to go (e.g., the philosophy and overall DNA of your children's ministry), but he won't make decisions about what happens in the trenches. He isn't involved in what happens on a day-to-day basis. For example, if a pastor says, "I want the Sunday school material to be gospel-centered," then you need to go out and find something that fits that priority. Then you will work to equip your teachers with how to communicate the curriculum in a developmentally appropriate way.
- *Option 3:* Your pastor says, "I want to be involved in everything." Your church-planting pastor wants to be engaged on both a macro and micro level of decision-making and preparation. He wants to set the big picture priorities but also be involved in the nitty-gritty details. With all that he has going on, it is unrealistic to expect him to review every step. Unless he is willing to delegate, you may need to decline serving in this role. Time constraints and stress levels dictate that church planters need help getting a new children's ministry started. Talk this through with your pastor and draw up a list of responsibilities required of a children's ministry leader. Once he sees your task list, he may be more willing to delegate. Try to envision for him our ideal option—option 2 ("I'll be involved at a macro level"). We think it's the wisest and most realistic choice.

2. Don't Assume the Church Planter's Wife Will Lead Children's Ministry

In the first year of many brand-new church plants, the pastor's wife is expected to organize and maintain their fledgling children's ministry. Most Sundays that means she is the children's ministry—*all of it*. She does the check-in. She organizes games and crafts. She watches the kids every week, as many volunteers are not yet reliable. She feeds the kids snacks. She changes dirty diapers and wipes noses.

Sadly, she rarely if ever participates in the public services, so she may go months without hearing her pastor (her husband) preach. She spiritually dries up. At the same time, she is overwhelmed by the demands of Sunday mornings. She keeps her spirits up, as she doesn't want to be a discouragement to her church-planting husband. But eventually—maybe about a year into the church plant—she realizes, "I can't keep doing this."

If you are the lead pastor in a church plant, don't let this be your wife. You might think this is a tall tale. This story isn't fiction; it's a real-life scenario that plays out in dozens of church plants. Dear pastor, don't let your wife's spiritual life suffer because she's given all of the responsibility for a start-up children's ministry. If your wife wants to help, that's great, but don't pile it all on her shoulders.

Let your wife be your wife, a mother, and a church member. Avoid making her the children's ministry director. That will do wonders for your marriage, let alone her sanity. And it will allow her to focus her time and attention where it belongs—on loving Jesus and encouraging you in your endeavors.

On the other hand, a pastor's wife occasionally serving in children's ministry can be of great value. Children's ministry service for a brand-new church plant is an "all hands on deck" endeavor. Your wife's participation will encourage your children's ministry leaders and provide a tangible means of support. Having your wife participate once a month also gives you feedback on the challenges in children's ministry, preventing you from becoming disconnected from this important ministry.

3. Start Small

The temptation is to try and launch a full-service children's ministry with offerings for every age level and creative programming from start to finish. The thinking goes like this—*if you build it, they will come*. If you create extra-big programs for kids, more families will stick around.

The danger is that you'll build an *unsustainable* program. It will burn out the few volunteers available, and you'll find yourself with the stress of filling in gaps to meet the demands of a large children's program. At first, some of your classes may look more like childcare than programmed discipleship for a few kids—that's okay. If the children are safe, the gospel is presented in their Bible story, and you don't lose a kid in your first six months, you are doing well.

Scale your start-up children's ministry to the size of what your start-up church can realistically handle. Then, as time goes on and as the church is blessed with more members, you can add to the children's ministry along the way.

4. Safety First

Dr. Anna Salters is the US's leading expert on sex offenders. She's done extensive interviews and research on their predatorial behavior. She writes, "I do not find that most pedophiles are looking for a challenge; most are looking for an easy target."[1]

Church plants are easy targets. Think with us for a moment about this. A church plant did a sex offender database search of every visitor to their church plant. They discovered three registered sex offenders attended in their first two and a half years. Remember, the vast majority of pedophiles haven't been caught and therefore are not registered.

Most church plants don't think carefully about child safety. They are inclined to quickly throw together a children's ministry—buy a curriculum, recruit a few volunteers, and then tell them to jump in headfirst. That's it.

Get your ministry leaders to write a child protection policy, screen volunteers with an application, and do background checks. But you may run into resistance. You might get comments like, "Why bother? We're a small group," or "We know everybody."

Don't give in to grumbling and opposition. Sex offenders presume that church plants will be an easy target because church planters have not thought carefully about how to create a safe environment for their children. There is easy access to children. After all, you'll probably be desperate for volunteers, right? If a self-professed believer shows up and he's energetic, kind, thoughtful, and helpful, you'll probably say, "Yes, please do jump in."

Don't be deceived. That's precisely what most sexual offenders want—to groom you (the gatekeeper) into thinking you should entrust the offender with opportunities to be around your church kids. Don't let your church plant be an easy target.

We want your church to be a radiant gospel witness for God's glory. Don't end up as a statistic in the *Houston Chronicle*—an example of yet another congregation that was careless about their kids and overrun by a covert abuser.

5. Don't Reinvent the Wheel

For church-planting pastors

One way your newly appointed leaders learn the administrative details is to shadow an experienced children's ministry director. Make arrangements for your start-up team to train under your sending church's children's ministry leaders. They can learn the main components of a children's ministry in a couple of weeks. But shadowing a children's ministry director for three to six months will expose your start-up team to the challenges and corresponding solutions that arise week to week.

If observing the children's ministry in your sending church is not an option, consider partnering with a gospel-preaching church in your community that you respect. Look for one that has a robust children's ministry that you'd like to model your work after. Call up their children's ministry director and ask him or her for a chance to talk about working with your leaders and allowing them to observe their ministry.

For the children's ministry leaders

Don't assume you can learn how to lead a children's ministry through phone calls. You can learn a lot about a program from a visit on a Sunday morning, but that isn't going to prepare or train you sufficiently.

The more experienced you are, the less time you'll need in training. But don't underestimate the value of an extended time serving alongside another ministry. For those with little or no experience, plan to observe another ministry for a minimum of two months, two or three Sundays per month. If you have the time, twice a month for a year will give you a base of knowledge and plenty of time to prepare your ministry plan.

Spend time in each of their different age-level programs. Ask questions about their philosophy of children's ministry; child safety policies and screening; volunteer recruitment and training; interactions with the church leadership; curriculum; the scope, sequence, structure, and flow of their children's programs; and the intersection between their children's ministry and the public services of the church, to name just a few things. Basically, ask them every question you can think up.

See if you can use their policy manual as a starting point for writing your own. Once you've drafted yours, ask the children's ministry director to read it over and make recommendations for changes.

Ask the leaders you are training under if they would be willing to do a walk-through of your meeting space as soon as one is identified. Having an experienced set of eyes can help you utilize the new space, flag potential security risks, and offer other suggestions.

Finally, as you observe and train alongside another ministry, think through and discuss the philosophical foundation for your ministry with your pastor. You'll want to work together to formulate your mission, vision, theme, and name in advance of your church plant launch and begin to pass this vision to your team.

6. Support Your Children's Ministry Team

How do you relate to your newly appointed children's ministry leaders? Regular communication is a must. Even if there is no meeting on the calendar, send a text or an email on Monday that asks, "How did it go yesterday? How are you? How can I pray for you?" Don't just settle for email and texting, however. Find periodic times to all meet in person and talk. Regular meetings give you a context to show support and direct the big-picture vision and philosophy.

Often a tension arises in a new church plant between children's ministry and the Sunday gathering. If your children's ministry does too much too early, half or more of your congregation will miss the preaching of the Word because they are serving in children's ministry. If you leave children's ministry with too few folks, you'll burn out your start-up team and perhaps compromise safety. Work with your children's ministry team ahead of time in order to strike a proper balance.

Most church plants need almost everyone to serve in children's ministry, which makes it a *whole church* endeavor. The church-planting pastor's support is crucial. His leadership envisions members joining in this task. "Come, serve in our children's ministry," he says, "Children are a blessing from the Lord, and we want to be faithful stewards of our kids."

If you as the pastor are both publicly and privately supportive, the children's ministry team will feel your support, which in turn will motivate them to work hard to make your children's ministry a success. Look for opportunities to encourage those serving in children's ministry and thank them for their service.

Appendix B
Guide to Writing and Implementing a Child Protection Policy

We don't want children abused or neglected. We want to faithfully steward the responsibility for our children. In order to do so, we must write a child protection policy (CPP). A CPP is a self-imposed set of standards that establishes a safe environment for our children. Some of your friends might say, "We don't need policies or procedures. We can just figure it out." Operating without a CPP is a recipe for disaster. If something does go wrong, you're left scrambling to deal with a big problem with little to no guidance. You improvise along the way, which exposes your lack of preparation.

If you agree that a CPP is a good thing, then how do you write and implement one? Beth Swagman advises, "No single policy works well everywhere! The child safety policy that works well in one church or nonprofit organization will not necessarily work well in another church or organization. Sample policies may help [you] visualize what the final product will look like, but an organization that adopts another organization's document without first examining how well it fits its own setting will often find that it should have 'tried it on before buying it.'"[1]

Rather than giving you sample policies, we think a better way to serve you is to identify the most important parts of a child protection policy and help you strategize how to best implement your new policy. We won't build the engine for you, but we can help you get started.

The Most Important Parts of a CPP

Let's start by tracing out the vital parts of a CPP and why they are important. The items included here are not comprehensive but are meant to give you a sense of what your CPP might include.

Lay out the vision and mission of children's ministry

The *vision* tells you where you want to go; the *mission* tells you how you are going to get there. What are the priorities, values, and goals for your children's ministry, and how do you want to accomplish them?

For example, our vision for children's ministry at Capitol Hill Baptist Church (CHBC) is "Generations of Godliness." When Christ returns, we want to be known as a church that raised up many generations of faithful believers to continue on with the great faith we have been given by our forefathers (Deuteronomy 6:4–9 and 2 Timothy 3:14–15).

Our mission states: The children's ministry of CHBC exists to glorify God by

- maintaining a safe and secure environment;
- supporting and encouraging parents who are primarily responsible for teaching biblical truths to their children (Ephesians 6:4);
- making the whole counsel of Scripture known to children with special emphasis on the gospel (Deuteronomy 6:6–9; Romans 1:16–17);
- praying for the children and relying on the Holy Spirit to regenerate their hearts through the faithful teaching of his Word (Romans 10:17; Ephesians 2:4–10);
- living faithfully before the children and modeling for them how Christians are called to respond to God

and interact with each other and the world around us (Matthew 5:16; 1 Corinthians 11:1);

- encouraging children to serve, not just be served (Mark 10:43–45);
- maintaining the highest ethical standards such that volunteers and teachers always live and serve above reproach, protecting the reputation of the gospel of Christ; and
- preparing children to participate in the Sunday gathering with their parents and, Lord willing, one day become a fully participating adult member.

Establish policy parameters

It is essential to define the parameters by which the policy does or does not apply. Defining the scope of the policy limits liability by helping to make clear what falls inside or outside the responsibility of the children's ministry staff or volunteers. For example, does the policy only apply to children's ministry events at the church or to offsite meetings like small groups too?

Know your state's laws

The laws of each state regarding the protection of children differ widely and are regularly changing. Some states, like Pennsylvania, require multiple background checks for all volunteers working with children. In our case at Covenant Fellowship, not just any online background check will do. We are required to secure an FBI fingerprint clearance, a Pennsylvania Child Abuse History Clearance, and a Pennsylvania State Criminal Background Check for every volunteer.

Don't assume local law enforcement will know the requirements for your church. They may not know the latest legislative changes. It is best to seek legal counsel to review your state's laws. An hour-long phone call with an attorney can help you understand your particular state's requirements. They can help ensure compliance for background checks, child abuse reporting requirements, and any other legal issues that can affect your classroom.

Define your personnel

Define who will participate in children's ministry, what their roles are, and what is required of them. For example, here's how one CPP defines personnel:

> *Staff* are the paid employees of the church. All full-time church staff are required to receive a background check, regardless of whether or not they have direct contact with children.
>
> *Volunteers* are those who work with children and are not employed by the church. All volunteers who serve in children's ministry are required to go through the children's ministry training and screening procedures before they serve. Volunteers include childcare workers, team leaders, hall monitors, teachers, and anyone else who serves the children.

Other personnel terms you might consider defining are "adults," "minors," "helpers," "deacons," "pastor/elders," or "governing body."

Set expectations for all staff and volunteers

If the personnel summary gives specific responsibilities for each role, this expectation section is more general. What general expectations do you have for everyone who serves? For example, a policy might say, "All children's ministry staff and volunteers share a responsibility for loving the children as Christ loves them and setting an example of proper Christian conduct in the way we live our lives."

Decide training and screening procedures

What training classes or screening procedures will the church employ? List them in this section. Some questions you might need to answer:

- How long should a person be a part of the church before he or she is allowed to serve alongside children?
- What is the minimum age of a volunteer?
- What kind of training do volunteers need to complete?
- Is there an application and is the volunteer required to fill it out?
- Will the church do background checks, reference checks, social media checks, or any other form of investigation into the person's past, like interviews or fingerprinting?
- Who approves the volunteers?
- What prior arrest record should prevent a person from serving with children?
- Will there be repeat checks in the future and how often?
- Is the staff required to undergo screening procedures?

Organize safe classroom settings

This includes the two-adult rule, specific adult-to-child ratios, guidelines for visibility, discipline, physical touch, and food and drink.

Two-adult rule. Because most child abusers like to hurt children in isolated settings, the experts recommend having two adults around at all times. To take it one step further, because family members are often unwilling to report wrongdoing by relatives, the experts also recommend two *unrelated* adults serving together. Also, specify any gender requirements (i.e., when two adults serve together, must one of them always be a woman?).

Adult-to-child ratios. What kind of ratios should you maintain to keep your kids safe? If you are not sure of this, call a local day care or school to find out what ratios they use.

Visibility. When classes or programs are in session, what is required? Do doors need to be open? What kind of visibility should those outside of the classroom have of the teacher and helpers?

Correction. When a child misbehaves, how should the staff, childcare workers, or teachers handle it? Trace out appropriate forms of correction and how they should be implemented.

Explain what ministry staff or volunteers are prohibited from doing. Be clear about what the volunteer should do if the child is out of control, likely to do harm to other children, or unresponsive to acceptable means of correction.

Communication. When, how, and for what reasons do staff and volunteers call parents to return for their children?

Physical touch. What is appropriate and inappropriate touch? Spell it out. Define this for both adult-to-child relationships and child- or teen-to-child relationships.

Changing diapers and proper bathroom assistance. Should any worker be permitted to change a diaper, or should you restrict that to women? Are volunteers permitted to help toddlers in the bathroom who require assistance? What is the proper procedure in dealing with bathroom accidents?

Food and drink. What is allowed and not allowed in the children's ministry areas? Will volunteers feed the youngest children, or are parents required to do this? Will the older kids get snacks and drinks? If so, what will they be served? How will allergies be handled? Are parents permitted to send snacks in with their children?

Provide protective rules and safety guidelines

What else do we need to do to keep our kids safe?

Sickness vs. wellness. Think through what the staff and volunteers must do to prevent infectious diseases. What should volunteers do when they change diapers, wipe noses, or handle blood spills? When should a child not participate in a classroom? What will the staff look for when they screen for sick children? How will toys and equipment be cleaned? This section should also include a description of universal precautions. See appendix C (page 188) for a sample communicable disease policy you can adapt to fit your needs.

Check-in and check-out process. What does a parent need to do to sign in a child and sign out a child? Describe what system is in place to accomplish this and how parents and volunteers use it. What happens if a parent loses the designated form of identification (e.g., wrist band or sticker)?

Restroom procedures. Explain who is allowed to take children to the restroom. Should you require a minimum of at least two children to go with an adult to the bathroom? Decide at what age a child is allowed to use the restroom on his or her own.

Transportation guidelines. Who is allowed to drive the children? How many adults and children or teens must be present to transport children or youth? What kind of consent is required by parents or anyone else who drives them? Should the driver keep a log of trips? How often will their driving record be reviewed? What state or federal requirement for a car seat, seat belt, or airbag safety should be stated in the policy? Does your auto insurance company allow nonstaff drivers of church vehicles?

Off-site or out-of-town event guidelines. Specify restrictions. For example, leaders should not be alone with children or teens. They have limits on physical contact. There is no dating between leaders and teens and no private communication apart from parental supervision. Additionally, there is and no alcohol or illegal drug use. Other things to consider might include the following:

- What is the minimum age difference between a volunteer/staff member and children or teens?
- What is the minimum number of staff or volunteers required to hold an off-site event?
- Is there a minimum number of children or teens required for an event or program?
- What should staff or volunteers do if a child's behavior warrants removal?
- What safety guidelines should the staff and volunteers adhere to when off-site? What kind of written consent is needed from parents? What sleeping arrangements should the kids have? Are children allowed to leave the site and, if so, under what conditions?
- What guidelines do you need for bathroom use or discipline during off-site or out-of-town events?

- What should volunteers or staff do in response to bullying?
- Do you need an insurance rider to cover your liability for the off-campus event?

Emergency response plan and evacuation procedures. How does the church plan to deal with an evacuation? A tornado or earthquake? An active shooter or some other security hazard? A missing child or a kidnapping? Responding to an active shooter and a tornado require different action plans.

A child-neglect and abuse-prevention reporting and response plan. Start by defining essential terms, like "abuse," "neglect," and so on. Define the steps a church should take to prevent abuse. Highlight who is the point of contact in handling abuse allegations and the guidelines for mandatory or nonmandatory (permissive) reporters. What are the state guidelines for reporting? What will the church do in response to allegations—report to police or Child Protective Services? Remove the alleged perpetrator from children's programs? Notify the congregation? Make sure the alleged perpetrator has a chaperone while at church? Suspend or fire a staff member? Specify what the church will do if it learns of allegations from the police or Child Protective Services. Also explain what kind of response the church will have if an adult alleges abuse when he or she was a child at the church. What are the parameters for confidentiality? How will the church handle the media?

Guidelines for how the church handles sex offenders who regularly attend or join your church. Clarify what the church will do if an offender attends the church one or two times. What if he or she starts to come regularly? Describe what happens if the offender decides to join the church. What kind of guidelines and prohibitions must the offender agree to before he joins the congregation?

A duty-to-warn policy. Will your church communicate with other churches, organizations, or schools about an abuser who once attended your church but is now attending their church or organization? If so, what does that process look like?

Add forms and resources

You can create an appendix in the back of your child protection policy for forms, lists, and other support resources. Consider including signs and symptoms of abuse; a sample of all children's ministry forms (incident report, medical consent, transportation consent); screening application (or any other type of application); and state guidelines for mandatory or permissive reports.

Strategy for Writing and Implementing a New CPP

If you are considering writing a child protection policy for the first time (or revising your existing CPP), you should think through the following steps.[2] You will probably have people who will resist your new policy, so pray and be patient through this process.

Review your church/denomination bylaws (or book of church order)

You will want to be sure to follow any requirements found in these governing documents. You may discover requirements or guidelines for protecting children already listed there.

Involve your church leadership from the start.

Find someone in church leadership who sees preventing and responding to child abuse as an important issue. Start a dialogue. Be gracious and thoughtful as you engage them. Begin with the concept of child abuse, the legal and moral obligations of protecting children, false assumptions, and possible fears or concerns.

You may field questions like, "Can abuse really happen at our church? Will a new policy be cumbersome and discourage people from serving in children's ministry? What legal parameters need to be considered?" or perhaps, "What helps the church to be prepared and reduce the risk of abuse?"

Equip the staff, volunteers, and the congregation.

Ignorance is one of the chief reasons why abusers are successful in church contexts, so educate your church about issues of child abuse. Use every means available to you to communicate with the church—special seminars, a Sunday sermon, bulletin inserts, articles in the church newsletter, and so on. As you educate and equip the congregation, you are also building consensus around the importance of this issue.

Write or rewrite your polices.

After the concept is approved by church leaders, someone has to do the hard work of writing a policy. Obtain sample copies of policies from other churches, but remember that every policy needs to be tailored to fit the specific needs of your church. Some churches like to form a committee that hammers out the details, but we've found that cumbersome and time-consuming. It is much more efficient for someone to be designated as a lead writer and then different church members (e.g., teachers, doctors, lawyers, nurses, parents) give feedback after the initial draft is finished. Then, you should have church leaders sign off on new policies and have the church's lawyers review it.

Train leaders, workers, and volunteers—and evaluate.

With a new policy in place, the church needs to be educated so that everyone is familiar with the new guidelines. Current workers need to be retrained, and new workers need to be trained before they serve for the first time. After some time is given to execute the policy, it should be evaluated by staff or church leaders. The children's ministry director can collect feedback from teachers and childcare workers and talk it over with the children's ministry leaders. If adjustments need to be made, revise the policy.

Maintain your policy.

Who is going to receive a copy of your policy? How often will you make changes? What is the process to get a policy change approved? Once you change the policy, who receives a copy of the amended document? How do you inform new members who join your church after your initial policy rollout is complete?

Appendix C
Communicable Disease Policy [Sample]

To prevent the spread of communicable diseases among children, the following guidelines are in place.

Children with infectious diseases should remain home until they are no longer contagious. A child should not participate in a class if and when any of the following exist:

- Fever, vomiting, or diarrhea (Note: Children should be free of a fever, vomiting, or diarrhea for twenty-four hours before coming to children's ministry.)
- Any symptoms of scarlet fever, German measles, mumps, chickenpox, or whooping cough, COVID-19, or influenza. Children should not return until cleared by medical personnel
- Common cold—from the onset of symptoms and one week thereafter
- Sore throat
- Croup
- Lice
- Any unexplained rash
- Any skin infection such as boils, ringworm, impetigo
- Pink eye or other eye infection
- Thick green, yellow, or constant nasal discharge
- Any other infectious disease

If a child exhibits any of these symptoms in the classroom after his or her arrival, he or she should be removed from contact with the other children and returned to the care of parents with an explanation of the symptoms.

During a more acute spread of disease, such as occurs in an outbreak or pandemic, it may be necessary to check children's temperatures and use hand sanitizer before receiving them into class. In these cases, follow the guidelines set in place by the Centers for Disease Control.

Volunteers will use disposable latex gloves and proper hygiene procedures to change diapers, wipe noses, and handle blood spills. Hand washing and the use of anti-bacterial hand sanitizer must be a regular habit for both children and volunteers.

Wash hands before and after any contact with bodily fluids, including wiping noses, changing diapers, cleaning vomit, and treating a blood spill. Always wear disposable gloves when dealing with any bodily fluids. Treat all soiled linen (i.e., sheets, clothing) as potentially infectious agents.

At the end of the day, disinfect the bathrooms and classroom and all toys with an antibacterial/antivirus cleaner or mist.

As a ministry dedicated to preventing the spread of disease among the children, your team leaders and the deacon/deaconess have the right to refuse a child based on questionable symptoms. To prevent the need to turn a child away from class participation, parents are asked to comply with the communicable disease policy guidelines.

Neither volunteers nor church staff may give any medication to any child.

Special Needs

Parents of children with special needs are encouraged to contact the children's ministry director *before* signing the child into class. This allows the staff to assess the child's needs and assist parents in transitioning their child into a classroom setting.

Appendix D
Recommended Resources

Resources by Marty Machowski

The Gospel Story Curriculum (A three-year Sunday School curriculum)

Long Story Short: 10-Minute Devotions to Draw Your Family to God

Old Story New: 10-Minute Devotions to Draw Your Family to God

The Gospel Story Bible: Discovering Jesus in the Old and New Testaments

Wise Up: Proverbs for the Classroom (A twelve-week curriculum)

Wise Up: 10-Minute Family Devotions in Proverbs

Listen Up: Jesus's Parables for Sunday School (A twelve-week curriculum)

Listen Up: 10-Minute Family Devotions on the Parables

Prepare Him Room: Celebrating the Birth of Jesus Advent Sunday School Curriculum (A four-week curriculum)

Prepare Him Room: Celebrating the Birth of Jesus Family Devotional

Note: All of the resources above work together to provide you with both a children's ministry curriculum and resources for family devotions at home.

The Ology: Ancient Truths Ever New (An illustrated systematic theology for kids)

Wonder Full: Ancient Psalms Ever New (A study of the book of Psalms with plenty of pictures and a fun fictional story)

God Made Me for Heaven: Helping Children Live for an Eternity with Jesus

God Made Boys and Girls: Helping Children Understand the Gift of Gender

Note: All of these resources are available at newgrowth press.com.

Additional Recommended Resources

Board Books

Jared Kennedy, *Jesus Rose for Me* (Greensboro, NC: New Growth Press, 2020).

Jared Kennedy, *Jesus Comes for Me* (Greensboro, NC: New Growth Press, 2020).

Jared Kennedy, *Jesus Is Bigger than Me* (Greensboro, NC: New Growth Press, 2021).

Sarah Reju, *God Is Better Than Trucks: An A-Z Alphabet Book* (Scotland, UK: Christian Focus Publications, 2017).

Sarah Reju, *Jesus Saves: The Gospel for Toddlers* (Greensboro, NC: New Growth Press, 2021).

Biographies

Catherine MacKenzie, *John Calvin: After Darkness Light* (Scotland, UK: Christian Focus Publications, 2009).

Catherine MacKenzie, *Martin Luther: Reformation Fire* (Scotland, UK: Christian Focus Publications, 2016).

Catherine MacKenzie, *John Knox: The Sharpened Sword* (Scotland, UK: Christian Focus Publications, 2012).

Rachel Lane, *John and Betty Stam: To Die is Gain* (Scotland, UK: Christian Focus Publications, 2021).

Nancy Drummond, *Lottie Moon: Changing China for Christ* (Scotland, UK: Christian Focus Publications, 2014).

Selah Helms, *Elizabeth Elliot: Do the Next Thing* (Scotland, UK: Christian Focus Publications, 2019).

Dave and Nate Jackson, *Hero Tales: A Family Treasury of True Stories From the Lives of Christian Heroes* (Minneapolis, MN: Bethany House Publishing, 1996).

Story Bibles

Jared Kennedy, *The Beginner's Gospel Story Bible* (Greensboro, NC: New Growth Press, 2017).

David Helm, *The Big Picture Story Bible* (Wheaton, IL: Crossway Publishing, 2014).

Missions

Rebecca Davis, *Living Water in the Dessert: True Stories of God at Work in Iran* (Scotland, UK: Christian Focus Publications, 2019).

Tim Keese and Peter Hansen (Directors), *Dispatches from the Front* (Frontline Missions International, DVD format).

Jason Mandryk, *Operation World: The Definitive Prayer Guide to Every Nation,* 7th ed. (Downers Grove, IL: Intervarsity Press, 2010).

Jason Mandryk and Molly Wall (Editors), *Window on the World: An Operation World Prayer Resource* (Downers Grove, IL: Intervarsity Press, 2018).

Family Devotions

Betsy Schmitt, *Sticky Situations: 365 Devotionals for Kids and Families* (Wheaton, IL: Tyndale House, 1997).

Sinclair Ferguson, *The Big Book of Questions and Answers: A Family Devotional Guide to the Christian Faith* (Scotland, UK: Christian Focus Publications, 2005).

Ann Hibbard, *Family Celebrations: Meeting Christ in Your Holidays and Special Occasions* (Brentwood, TN: Wolgemuth & Hyatt, Publishers, 1988).

Sally Michael, *God's Names* (Phillipsburg, NJ: P&R Publishing, 2011).

Corlette Sande, *The Young Peace Maker: Teaching Students to Respond to Conflict God's Way* (Wapwallopen, PA: Shepherds Press, 1997).

Champ Thornton, *The Radical Book for Kids* (Greensboro, NC: New Growth Press, 2016).

Picture Books

Susan Hunt, *Sammie and His Shepherd: Seeing Jesus in Psalm 23* (Lake Mary, FL: Reformation Trust Publishing, 2008).

R. C. Sproul, *The Priest with Dirty Clothes* (Lake Mary, FL: Reformation Trust Publishing, 2011).

Fiction with Christian Themes

Patricia St. John, *Rainbow Garden* (Chicago, IL: Moody Publishers, 2002).

Patricia St. John, *Treasures of the Snow* (Chicago, IL: Moody Publishers, 2001).

Patricia St. John, *The Tanglewoods' Secret* (Chicago, IL: Moody Publishers, 2001).

Patricia St. John, *Star of Light* (Chicago, IL: Moody Publishers, 2002).

Patricia St. John, *The Secret of Pheasant Cottage* (Chicago, IL: Moody Publishers, 2002).

Child Safety

Justin and Lindsey Holcomb, *God Made All of Me: A Book to Help Children Protect Their Bodies* (Greensboro, NC: New Growth Press, 2015).

Acknowledgments

I (Deepak) thank Marty, first of all, for being willing to write this book with me. Years ago when I was a young duckling, I approached Marty with questions, and time and again, he patiently answered, mentored, and showed kindness to me. He's been a picture of grace—God's undeserved favor—that I didn't and still don't deserve. I knew this book would be much better if the readers had a seasoned veteran like Marty, someone who has walked through the highs and lows of children's ministry for over three decades!

Thank you also to our amazing children's ministry trio at Capitol Hill Baptist Church—Gio, Susan, and Connie—without whom I would be in trouble. Technically, I could have footnoted every page with their three names on it. Thank you for your love and encouragement over so many years. Thank you also to a long line of deacons who have been a wonderful support to our children's ministry.

Thank you to the elders of Capitol Hill Baptist Church and the congregation for so many years of encouragement.

Thank you, finally, to my dear wife, Sarah, and our five kids, Zac, Lydia, Eden, Noelle, and Abe. Little does the church know that they're indebted to you—for helping to shape, refine, and inspire me to be a better shepherd leader. I love you, and I'm a much richer man because of you.

* * *

I (Marty) can remember Deepak first inviting me to participate in a conference call with a few of his children's ministry director friends from across the country. His leadership and wisdom in seeing the importance of sharing challenges and fellowshipping with other children's ministry leaders helped me and my ministry grow and mature. I treasure our friendship, and writing this book together has been a joy and delight.

Like Deepak, I've had a team of folks advancing the work of ministry to children at Covenant Fellowship. Many thanks go out to the couples who have led our ministry through the years. Tim and Cindy Campbell got us started, Dwayne and Tony Bennett brought us into our new building. Kevin and Crystal Zepp and Jeff and Erin Cassel took the baton from the Bennetts and gave us hours and hours of their time to help us continue, improve, and grow.

I'd like to also thank the elders of Covenant Fellowship for their unwavering support and my wife, Lois, for her example in serving in Promise Kingdom for the past thirty years. Her feedback, suggestions, and encouragement kept me going and improving. To my children, Emma, Nathan, Martha, Noah, Anna, and Amelia, thanks for serving as my object lesson test pilots, camera operators, and all-around helpers. I pray God will pour out his grace upon you to pass on the joy of Christ to your children.

* * *

From both of us: Thank you to Barbara, Ruth, and the team at New Growth Press for your encouragement. Your gospel-centered commitments are continually inspiring. Thank you also to first-draft readers Gio Lynch, Susan Wall, Jenny Apple, and Kevin and Crystal Zepp. You made the book better through your feedback! Thank you also to editor Ivan Mesa, who cleaned up the manuscript and helped us convert any underwhelming introductions or conclusions to stories that encourage and inspire.

Endnotes

Chapter 1

1. I (Deepak) have heard Connie Dever make this point about Bunyan many times in seminars at our children's ministry workshops.

Chapter 5

1. If you want to think more about deacons in the local church, see Matt Smethurst's *Deacons: How They Serve and Strengthen the Church* (Wheaton, IL: Crossway, 2021).

2. For more on membership, see Jonathan Leeman's excellent book *Church Membership: How the World Knows Who Represents Jesus* (Wheaton, IL: Crossway, 2012).

Chapter 6

1. Thanks to Gio Lynch for helping me with this paragraph.

2. Thanks to Gio Lynch for help with this paragraph.

3. You can learn more about this active shooter training at https://www.alicetraining.com/.

4. For more information about sexual abuse prevention and response training, check out https://ministrysafe.com/.

Chapter 7

1. *ESV Study Bible* (Wheaton, IL: Crossway, 2008), 1033.

2. We were helped by Peter Leithart's thoughtful article "3 Ways to Teach Scripture to Children," The Gospel Coalition, November 11, 2019, https://www.thegospelcoalition.org/article/teach-scripture-children/.

3. Leithart, "3 Ways to Teach Scripture to Children."

Chapter 8

1. Much of the content of this chapter comes from Deepak Reju, *On Guard: Preventing and Responding to Child Abuse at Church* (Greensboro, NC: New Growth Press, 2014).

2. Gavin de Becker, foreword to Anna Salter, *Predators, Pedophiles, Rapists, and Other Sex Offenders: Who They Are, How They Operate, and How We Can Protect Ourselves and Our Children* (New York: Basic Books, 2003), xi.

3. de Becker, foreword to Salter, *Predators*, xi.

4. Jaycee Dugard, *A Stolen Life: A Memoir* (New York: Simon & Schuster, 2011), 9–11.

5. Dugard, *A Stolen Life*, 9–11.

6. Howard N. Snyder, *Sexual Assault of Young Children as Reported to Law Enforcement: Victim, Incident, and Offender Characteristics*, NIBRS Statistical Report (US Department of Justice, July 2000), 10, https://www.bjs.gov/content/pub/pdf/saycrle.pdf. The victim-offender relationship in sexual assault for ages five and under: 48.6 percent from a family member, 48.3 percent from acquaintance, and 3.1 percent from a stranger.

7. James Cobble, Richard Hammer, and Steven Klipowicz, *Reducing the Risk II: Making Your Church Safe From Sexual Abuse* (Carol Stream, IL: Church Law & Tax Report, 2003), 12.

8. Salter, *Predators*, 76–78.

9. Salter, *Predators*, 38.

10. Victor Vieth, "What Would Walther Do? Applying the Law and Gospel to Victims and Perpetrators of Child Sexual Abuse," *Journal of Psychology and Theology* 40, no. 4 (December 2012): 263.

11. Salter, *Predators,* 42.

12. Carla Van Dam, *Identifying Child Molesters: Preventing Sexual Abuse by Recognizing the Patterns of the Offenders* (New York: Routledge, 2011), 110–12.

13. Vieth, "What Would Walther Do?," 263.

14. Van Dam, *Identifying Child Molesters*, 104, emphasis added.

15. Salter, *Predators*, 43.

16. Van Dam, *Identifying Child Molesters*, 77.

17. I (Deepak) learned this from Greg Love and Kimberly Norris through the basic training. For more information about training through ministry safe, visit https://www.ministrysafe.com.

18. Reju, *On Guard*.

19. Available at https://ministrysafe.com/.

Chapter 9

1. James Cobble, Richard Hammer, and Steven Klipowicz, *Reducing the Risk II: Making Your Church Safe From Sexual Abuse* (Carol Stream, IL: Church Law & Tax Report, 2003), 42–44.

2. Cobble, Hammer, and Kilpowicz, *Reducing the Risk II*, 41–44.

3. To see more about membership in a church, see Jonathan Leeman's excellent book *Church Membership: How the World Knows Who Represents Jesus* (Wheaton, IL: Crossway, 2012).

4. Cobble, Hammer, and Klipowicz, *Reducing the Risk II*, 32.

5. We learned this from Kimberly Norris in the Ministry Safe Basic Training. See also https://ministrysafe.com/the-safety-system/background-checks/.

Chapter 10

1. See Church Mutual Insurance's *Fire Safety in Your Worship Center*, https://www.churchmutual.com/media/pdf/fire_safety.pdf. See also "Our Top Church Fire Safety Tips—Keep Your Congregation Safe!," Dial My Calls, accessed January 7, 2021, https://www.dialmycalls.com/blog/top-10-fire-safety-tips-church.

2. "Fire Safety: Create an Evacuation Plan Before an Emergency Happens," Brotherhood Mutual, accessed January 7, 2021, https://www.brotherhoodmutual.com/resources/safety-library/risk-management-articles/disasters-emergencies-and-health/fire-safety-and-prevention/fire-safety-create-an-evacuation-plan-before-an-emergency-happens/.

3. See *Fire Safety in Your Worship Center*, 2. See also Brotherhood Mutual's "Fire Safety: Create an Evacuation Plan Before an Emergency Happens."

4. "You should have at least one extinguisher for every 2,500 square feet, with a minimum of one extinguisher on each level of your

building. . . ." Check your local fire code and get an inspection to make sure you are meeting the requirements for fire safety in your community. See Church Mutual Insurance Company, *Fire Safety in Your Worship Center*.

5. Adapted from *Fire Safety in Your Worship Center*.

6. An extinguisher should be within a seventy-five foot distance of any spot within the children's area.

7. We got this phrase ("Plan a Great Escape") from Brotherhood Mutual's "Fire Safety: Create an Evacuation Plan Before an Emergency Happens."

8. Brotherhood Mutual, "Fire Safety: Create an Evacuation Plan Before an Emergency Happens."

9. "Charts and Maps," Gun Violence Archive, accessed January 23, 2021, https://www.gunviolencearchive.org.

10. "Active Shooter Attacks: Security Awareness for Soft Targets and Crowded Places," Homeland Security, accessed January 23, 2021, https://www.fema.gov/sites/default/files/2020-03/fema_faith-communities_active-shooter.pdf.

11. "Active Shooter: What You Can Do," FEMA, accessed January 23, 2021, https://emilms.fema.gov/IS0907/curriculum/1.html.

12. Alice Training, https://www.alicetraining.com.

Chapter 11

1. Thank you to a group of stellar professional teachers—Sarah Chen, Alina Banu, Lauren Wolfe, Jennilee Miller, and Allison Kaczowka—who answered questions to help us build this chapter.

2. This idea of lenient teachers being walked over by kids comes from personal correspondence with Sarah Chen (January 4, 2021).

3. This idea comes from personal correspondence with Sarah Chen (January 4, 2021).

4. This paragraph is based off of correspondence with Allison Kaczowka (January 4, 2021).

5. This comes from personal correspondence with Alina Banu (January 4, 2021).

6. Doug Lemov, *Teach Like a Champion 2.0: 62 Techniques that Put Students on the Path to College* (San Francisco: Josse-Basse, 2015), 388.

7. Lemov, *Teach Like a Champion*, 388.

8. Lemov, *Teach Like a Champion*, 390, 402–3.

9. Lemov, *Teach Like a Champion*, 394.

10. These examples are adapted from the examples in Lemov, *Teach Like a Champion*, 394.

11. This teaching tip comes from personal correspondence with Jennilee Miller (January 4, 2021).

12. Lemov, *Teach Like a Champion*, 395–96.

13. Lemov, *Teach Like a Champion*, 397.

14. This teaching tip comes from personal correspondence with Alina Banu (January 4, 2021).

15. Lemov, *Teach Like a Champion*, 398.

16. Lemov, *Teach Like a Champion*, 399.

17. This teaching tip comes from personal correspondence with Alina Banu (January 4, 2021).

18. Lemov, *Teach Like a Champion*, 400–402.

19. Lemov, *Teach Like a Champion*, 401–2.

20. Lemov, *Teach Like a Champion*, 402–3.

21. Lemov, *Teach Like a Champion*, 403.

22. Lemov, *Teach Like a Champion*, 405.

23. Lemov, *Teach Like a Champion*, 404.

24. This teaching tip comes from personal correspondence with Jennilee Miller (January 4, 2021).

25. This example comes from personal correspondence with Sarah Chen (January 4, 2021).

26. This teaching tip comes from personal correspondence with Jennilee Miller (January 4, 2021).

27. This example comes from personal correspondence with Alina Banu (January 4, 2021).

Appendix A

1. Anna Salter, *Predators: Pedophiles, Rapists, and Other Sex Offenders: Who They Are, How They Operate, and How We Can Protect Ourselves and Our Children* (New York: Basic Books, 2003), 225.

Appendix B

1. Beth Swagman, *Preventing Child Abuse: Creating a Safe Place* (Grand Rapids, MI: Faith Alive Christian Resources, 2009), 17.

2. James Cobble, Richard Hammer, and Steven Klipowicz, *Reducing the Risk II: Making Your Church Safe From Sexual Abuse* (Carol Stream, IL: Church Law & Tax Report, 2003), 67–71.